C00 4531957X
EDINBURGH LIBRARII
D0192088

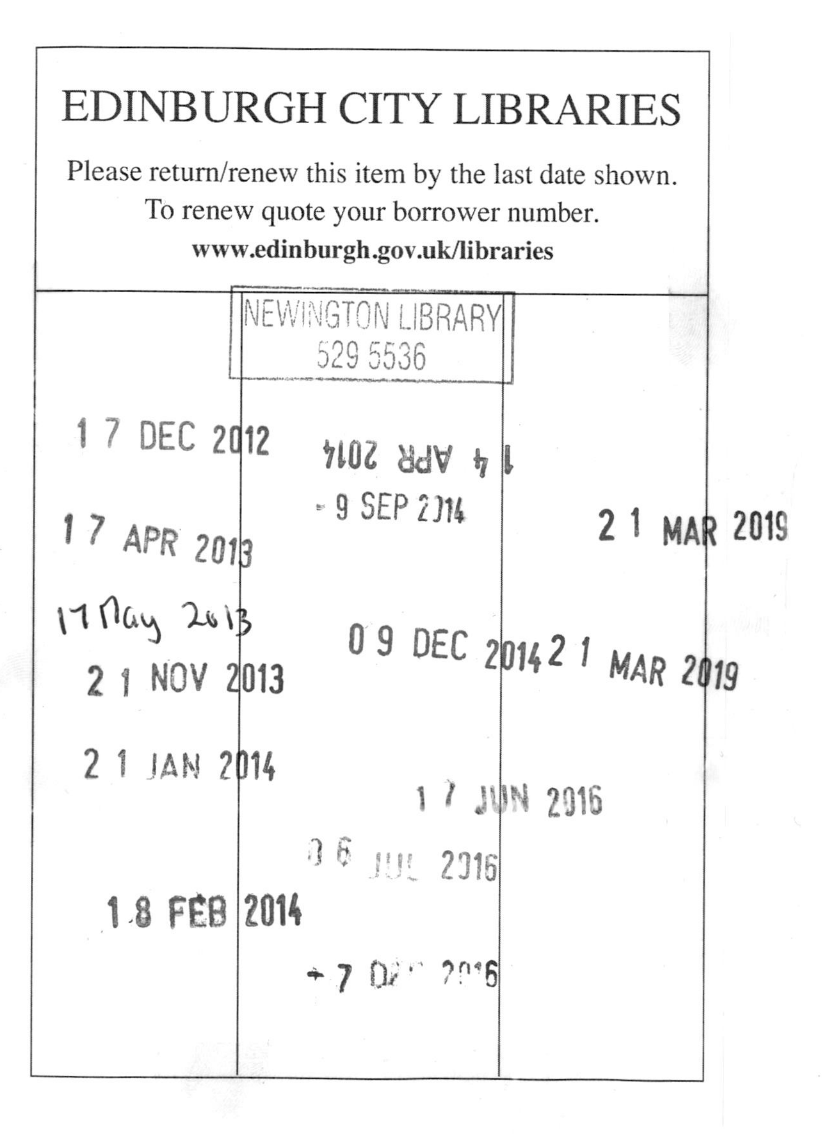

Knitty Gritty

The next steps

by Aneeta Patel

photography by Peter Schiazza

B L O O M S B U R Y
LONDON • NEW DELHI • NEW YORK • SYDNEY

Dedication

This book is dedicated to Everyone

Thank You and thank Me

First published in Great Britain in 2012

Reprinted in 2012

Bloomsbury Publishing Plc
50 Bedford Square
London WC1B 3DP

www.bloomsbury.com

ISBN: 978-1-4081-3132-9

CIP Catalogue records for this book are available from the British Library and the U.S. Library of Congress.

Commissioning editor: Susan James
Project manager: Agnes Upshall
Cover design: Sutchinda Rangsi Thompson
Page layout: Susan McIntyre
Photography: Peter Schiazza

This book is produced using paper that is made from wood grown in managed, sustainable forests. It is natural, renewable and recyclable. The logging and manufacturing processes conform to the environmental regulations of the country of origin.

Printed and bound in Italy

Acknowledgements

Invaluable in my work are my fabulous test knitters and students who've tried and tested my patterns and workshops. Guinea pigs – Abi Dove, Alex Mclean, Alison Forsythe, Amelia Healey, A. Goga, Caroline Fenton, Catherine Alaguiry, Catherine Esland, Cetra Coverdale, Charlotte Saunders, Cheryl Williams, David Withington, Dawn Bray, Debbie Coughlin, Ellen Grace, Ellen Parnavelas, Fionne Harrington, Grace Edghill, Giulietta Driver, Harriet Tenenbaum, Hayley Dalton, Helen Wakeley, Jane Freimiller, Jane Wilson, Jayne Morgan, Jennifer Hill, Jill Petty, Karen Blair, Karla Hammond, Kate Bullas, Kate Shurety, Kathryn Matthews, Kaye Archer, Kylie Archer, Linda Hill, Mary Cowin, Megan Kelly, Michelle Ryan, Natalie Billington, Niki Stevens, Owen Pearson, Rhiann Thompson, Rowena Hill, Ruth Ball, Samantha Bell, Sarah Hook, Seb Arnold, Seeta Patel, Sim Burton, Sue Richards, Summer Mughrabi, Sybil Caines, Vicky Cowin and Wendy Meteyard – thank you so much!

Thank you to everyone involved in the photo shoots (it's not that easy modelling knitwear in the summer!): Alexis Larusson, Alix Stredwick, Amelie Blair, Ava James, Beatrice Roberts, Ben Neuville, Caroline Fenton, Carrie Cracknell, Catherine Alaguiry, Chris & Yvonne Abbess, Eva Karkut-Law, Eva Larusson, Jane Freimiller, Jemima Roberts, Jess Schiazza, Jonathan Allen, Karen Blair, Lauren Neuville, Lilia Larusson, Lucy Neuville, Owen Pearson, Peter Brownell, Peter Schiazza, Poppy Blair, Rachel Weatherup, Robin Priestley, Rowena Hill, Summer Mughrabi and her lovely flat, Susan Neuville, Tracy Karkut-Law and the flat I want to live in, Wendy Meteyard and Woody Brownell.

So many people helped make this book possible and coped with my numerous trials, tribulations and tantrums. My grateful thanks go to my parents, for the example they set and for showing me the person I aim to be; all my students, for fuelling my passion for creating; Susan James and Peter Schiazza, for having enough faith to go through it all again; Owen Pearson for the OPMs; everyone within cycling distance, for turning up to help whenever I panicked; and not forgetting me, for being allergic to wool fibres and continuing to be me even when it wasn't a comfortable thing.

Sponsors

Yarn and other materials were kindly donated by the generous people at:

Stylecraft
discover, create and enjoy

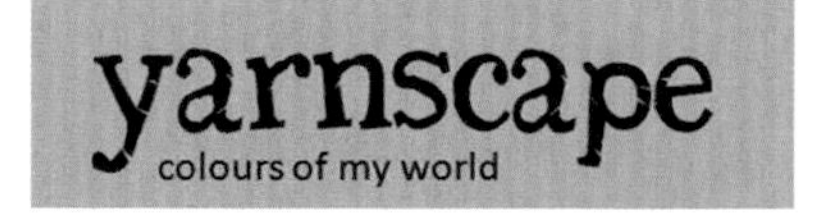

artesano
hummingbird
100%
Debbie Bliss
alpaca silk aran
25039
02818
the knit kit
ROWAN
Pure Wool DK
SIRDAR
click
double knitting with wool
SIRDAR
click
Stylecraft
DOUBLE KNITTING
Susan Bates
9.0
10.0
Sublime
bamboo & pearls

Contents

ROWAN
Pure Wool DK

Introduction

As with my first book, *Knitty Gritty: Knitting for the Absolute Beginner*, everything has been tried and tested by advanced-beginner and intermediate knitters, who have played an essential part in making this a user-friendly guide to the next stage in your knitting know-how.

I hope you enjoy the ride!

So ... you've knitted approximately 111 scarves, a few odds and ends, and been thoroughly baffled by a pattern written in Martian (I mean 'the ancient language of Knit') for a stylish little cardie that would be perfect if it were a little bit longer, had three-quarter-length sleeves and was stripy. Welcome to The Next Step in your knitting career! I'm Aneeta and I will be your guide in this tour of everything from mysterious knitting abbreviations to three-needle bind-offs to short-row shaping. We will be stopping off at the Stitch Library for a group hug and there is an optional detour to Sock City.

I plan to warm you up with some beguilingly simple patterns that will teach you a few essentials of shaping and finishing, and then throw you head-first into the excitement of double-pointed needles, giving patterns a personal touch, and a few other SSKs and SKPOs.

Tension and gauge

Knitting tension (or the gauge of your knitting) can seem like a mathematical minefield when you first learn about it. What it means is ensuring that you knit the same sized piece, with the same number of stitches as in a knitting pattern, to make a garment the same size as the one shown.

Tension is less important for projects like scarves, shawls and bags, as these don't need to have an exact fit. But they are very important to consider if you are knitting a garment with a fitted shape. If your tension isn't accurate, you might do a lot of knitting only to end up with a garment that's too big or too small, which would be very annoying!

This can be tricky, as we all knit tighter or looser than the knitter next to us, and I've found that this often trips up less experienced knitters, but it can be important, so I'll try to explain it.

Most gauges are measured in stocking stitch, but they can also be specific to the stitch used in an individual pattern. I'll explain it for stocking stitch – but the principle is the same for all stitches.

Gauges are usually measured in stitches per 10cm. This means how many stitches (and rows) you need to knit to end up with a square that measures 10 x 10cm. For example, using double knit yarn and 4mm needles, the standard tension is 22sts x 30 rows = 10cm square of stocking stitch. This means that if you cast on 22sts and knit in stocking stitch for 30 rows, you should end up with a 10cm square of knitting.

Every knitting pattern states the tension required in terms of a small sample square of knitting called a tension square, which you should knit before you start to check that you are working to the correct tension.

It is suggested that every time you use a new yarn to knit a garment that needs to fit precisely, you work a tension square before you start. As I said, although a gauge for the yarn will be shown at the start of most knitting patterns, it's not essential to work a tension square for items like toys, scarves, etc. that don't need a precise fit. If you are knitting a scarf that asks for double knit yarn for example, you can confidently use any double knit yarn available for this non-fitted project.

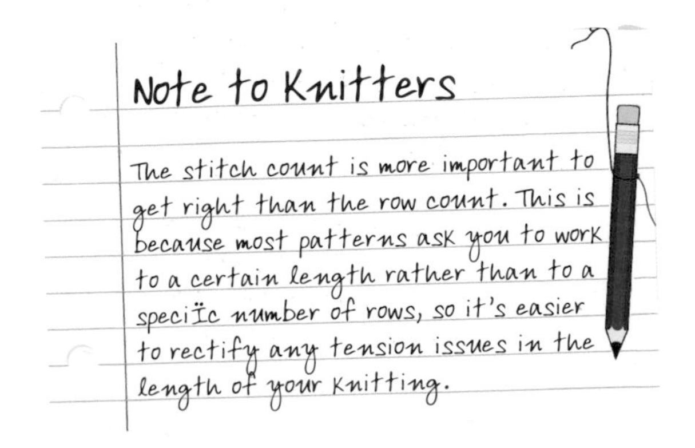

Learn to read the information on the yarn label. It will tell you the optimum needle size and the gauge, as well as useful stuff such as washing instructions. You might find it useful to start a scrapbook for your knitting projects, and stick in the yarn label and a bit of the yarn for each pattern.

However, if you are about to embark on a garment that is shaped, and needs to fit, a tension square is recommended. Here are a few things to remember when knitting a tension square:

1. When you are working a tension square, start by casting on around 10 more stitches than the gauge asks for. This way, you can measure the stitches in the middle of the square and get a more accurate measurement than if measuring right to the ends of a knitted piece.

2. For the same reason, work a few more rows than the gauge specifies, so you aren't measuring right to the edge.

3. If your square works out to be smaller than it should be, you need to work another tension square using bigger needles (start with 1mm bigger).

4. If the square ends up bigger than it should be, your tension is too loose and you need to try again with smaller needles.

Questions & Answers

Help! I've counted the right number of stitches but not the right number of rows.

Getting the stitch count right is more important than getting the right number of rows. This is because most patterns tell you to knit to a certain length, rather than a specific number of rows.

I've counted 18sts within my 10cm square and not 14sts as the yarn label says.

If you have more stitches than you should have, your tension is too tight. If you have fewer stitches than you should have, your tension is too loose. If the tension is too tight, re-knit the square using bigger needles (or smaller needles if the tension is too loose).

How to measure the gauge of a tension square

Step 1: Using the recommended needles for your yarn, knit a practice square about 10sts and 10 rows bigger than the tension square shown on the yarn label. For example, the gauge for the yarn in the photo is 14sts x 22 rows in stocking stitch on 7mm needles = 10cm square. Therefore I knitted my tension square to 24sts and 32 rows.

Step 2: Then pin out a section 10cm square. The area you've measured out should contain 14sts x 22 rows.

Note to Knitters

Some knitting projects, such as scarves, blankets and toys, will not be too badly affected if your tension is slightly off. The time to be concerned is if you are knitting a precisely fitted garment. But as with everything, don't worry too much. Figuring out tension will take a bit of getting used to and you'll need to exercise your maths muscles, but you'll work it out. As I'll tell you again and again in this book, be patient.

A tension square isn't always necessary for children's garments; you can always knit one size bigger for a child if you want to be on the safe side.

The projects

I hope you find the size you're looking to knit in the projects shown in my book. Whilst I've tried to accommodate small, medium and large sizes for most of the garments, this is primarily a book for you to learn some intermediate techniques, and how to understand patterns in general. So if you don't find the size you need here, then hopefully the skills you learn whilst working on my projects will give you the knowledge and confidence to try all of the myriad of patterns to be found in other books and on the Internet.

The techniques and tips you'll learn whilst knitting the projects in this book are designed to give your work personality and finesse, and to give you as a knitter the confidence to be individual and brave in your knitting choices.

Please remember that my aim is to teach you some intermediate knitting skills and give you belief in yourself as a knitter. Then you can go forth and tackle some of the 'trendier' patterns you'll find out there in the wider knitting world!

Handy
HINT

Substituting yarn
If the pattern says to use a specific yarn that you can't find or don't wish to use (for example, I'm allergic to pure wool so always try to find a cotton or man-made alternative), then checking your gauge by knitting a tension square will help you in making the correct choice of yarn for your pattern. Always take the pattern with you when shopping for yarn, as knitting shop staff have lots of practice in yarn substitution.

Choosing your yarn (The Science Bit)

Rather than following the traditional knitting pattern route of saying exactly which brand of yarn you must use for a pattern, I will be giving you options and instructions so you can work within the correct gauge and weight of yarn, but be more creative and flexible with the yarn you choose, to suit you and your budget. The way I've done this is to give an approximate metreage of yarn required, rather than going by weight. Different fibres have different weights. For example, cotton is lighter than wool, so a 50g ball of cotton will have a longer metreage than a 50g ball of pure wool. So rather than tell you to use, say, 100g of a specific yarn, I will state the approximate metreage you'll need to work at a specific gauge. Then you can read the yarn labels, which all describe the metreage as well as the weight, and choose a yarn with the correct gauge to go with the pattern.

For example:
For the Adult booties on p.48, you need 107m yarn, 10mm needles, and a tension of 9sts for a 10cm square knitted in stocking stitch. A yarn that will knit up to that gauge is Rowan Big Wool, and there are 80m in each 100g ball of that wool. Here's the Science Bit:

Total number of metres needed for the project
÷ the number of metres in the ball of yarn
= the number of balls of yarn you need.

For the Adult booties, the maths would be:

107m (the amount needed for a pair of booties)
÷ 80m (the metreage in one ball of Rowan Big Wool)
= 1.34

So you need approximately 1.34 balls of Rowan Big Wool to knit a pair of Adult booties. Of course you would need to buy two balls and would have a bit left over at the end.

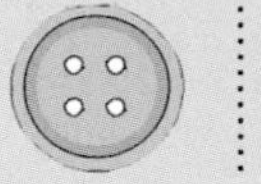

***Handy* HINT**

Have another read of the section on tension and gauge (see p.12) if you need a refresher on the maths involved. Hopefully my working out of the metreage will make your life easier if you aren't a natural boffin – I am definitely not, so I got plenty of help with working out my knitting maths!

Well done to you all for sticking with me through the maths part!

My method is not the traditional way of showing yarn quantities for a pattern, but I hope that it will make your knitting choices more fluid and less prescribed, thus adding to the individuality of your knitting. It'll mean a little more maths for you at the start, but in the long run it will mean that you get to make more creative decisions in your knitting.

How to use this book

The main thing to remember is that this book aims to teach you and give you confidence in your knitting. Follow the techniques chapters carefully, and if some practice is suggested, then please do it – it will benefit you in the long run, I promise! When you come to try out the projects, if you are a less confident knitter, follow the patterns as written. If you are more confident or become more confident as you work through the book, feel free to adapt the patterns to suit you. Be brave and you'll learn so much more about knitting than you can learn from any book! Don't be afraid to experiment: I've learnt more from the mistakes I've made in my knitting than from following every pattern exactly as it is written.

I hope that I've given you enough information to guide you, but not so much that you won't be able to use your initiative to progress further. Once you've mastered the techniques, you can be as creative as you dare!

Techniques

Casting on

There are lots of different ways to cast on, but here are two of the most used methods. Sometimes a pattern will suggest a particular method, and at other times you are free to experiment and find out which method you like the best.

Basic two-needle cast-on

I find this the simplest method for less experienced knitters, as it has many of the same moves as the basic knit stitch.

Step 1: Start with the slip knot on the left-hand needle and pick up the stitch with the right-hand needle, pushing the tip through to the back so that the needles are crossed left over right. Hold both the needles in your left hand.

Step 2: Wrap the yarn back and then middle around the right-hand needle (the one that's crossed at the back).

Step 3: Push the tip of the right-hand needle into the loop on the left-hand needle, under and to the front of the work.

Step 4: Stand the needles up straight and hold the stitches with your thumbs.

Step 5: Insert the tip of the left-hand needle up into the stitch on the right.

Step 6: Release (pull out) the right-hand needle out of the stitch: you have cast on a new stitch.

Continue until you have as many stitches as you need.

Thumb method

You might find that you get a neater edge if you use the thumb method, if you are starting with a ribbed border, or you might just prefer it to the two-needle cast-on. Have a go and start learning about your own preferences.

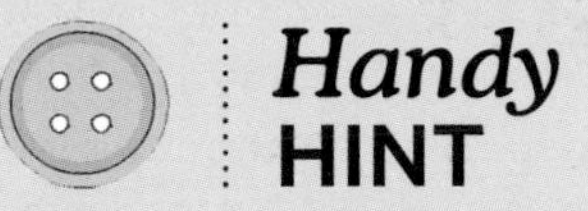

Handy HINT

It's always hard to tell how much yarn to leave in the long tail of yarn. Be cautious: leave as much as you think you need and then add a bit more! It's very frustrating if you cast on lots of stitches and run out of yarn just before you have the number you need. A good tip is to cast on 10sts and see how much yarn that uses. You can then do a bit of maths to multiply it to the amount you need, and add on a bit for luck. Think more, rather than less!

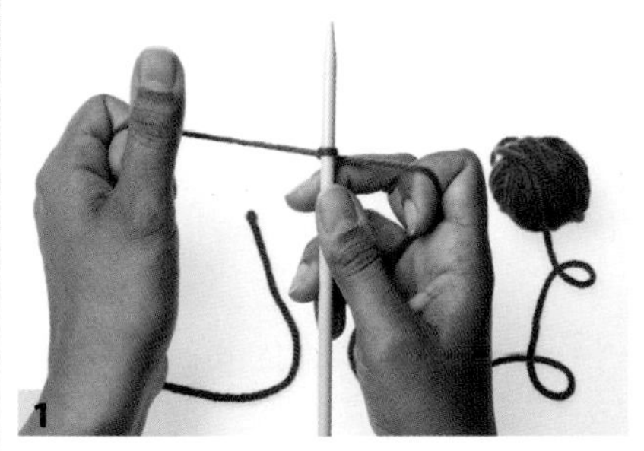

Step 1: Make a slip knot, leaving a long tail of yarn. This long tail will be needed to make the cast-on stitches, so make sure you leave plenty.

Hold the needle with the slip knot in your right hand. Keep the yarn attached to the ball in your right hand, and the long tail of yarn in your left hand.

Stand your left thumb so it is facing upwards, holding the long tail of yarn behind your thumb.

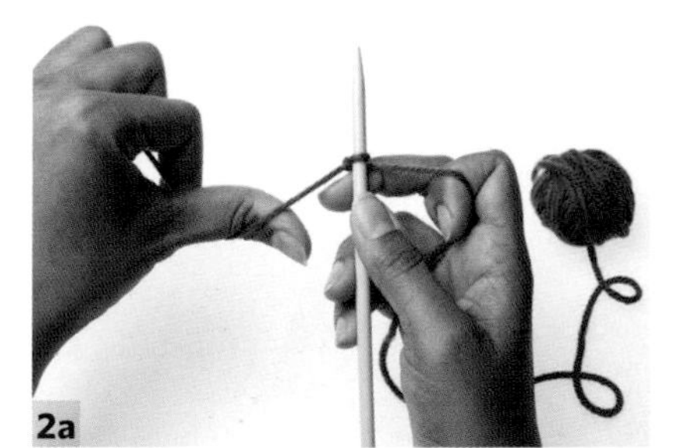

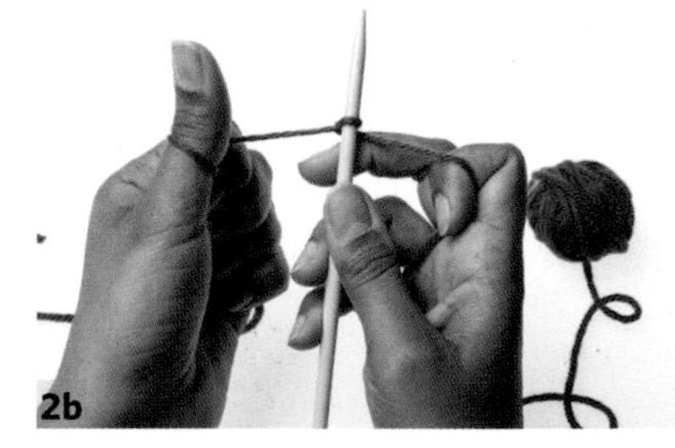

Step 2: Put your left thumb under and up the long end of the yarn.

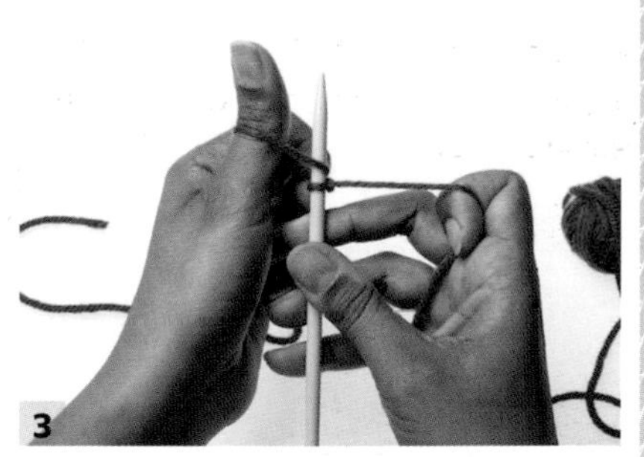

Step 3: Put the needle up the yarn you've wrapped around your left thumb.

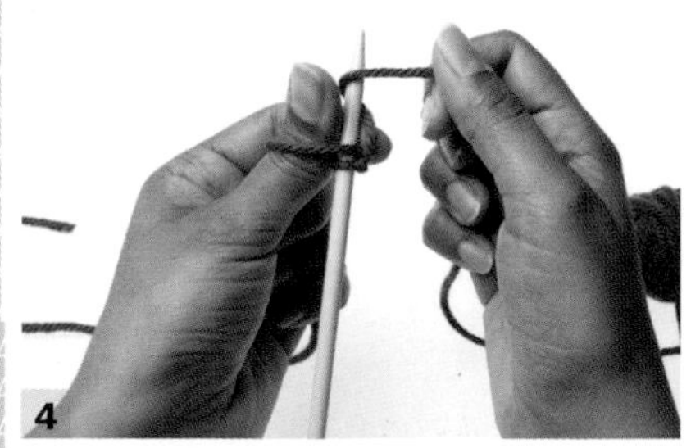

Step 4: Move the needle to your left hand and wrap the yarn that's attached to the ball back and then middle around the needle, using your right hand.

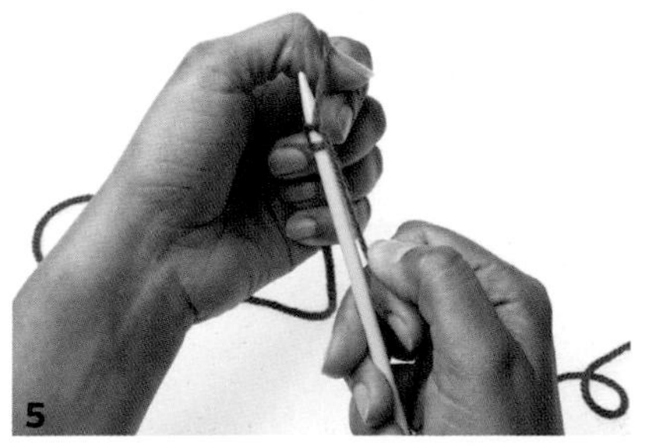

Step 5: Move the needle back over to your right hand and lift the yarn wrapped around your left thumb over the needle.

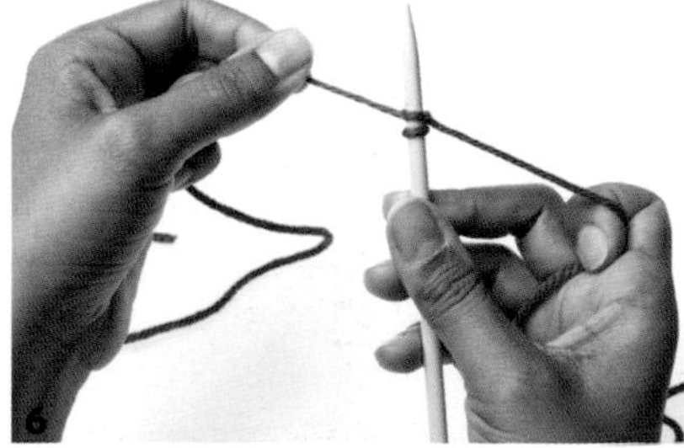

Step 6: Release the yarn from your left thumb and pull tightly on both ends of the yarn.

Continue until you have the number of stitches you require.

Basic stitches

Knitting is made up of two basic stitches: knit and purl. Using them in different combinations gives you different effects. Let's brush up on the basics.

Note to Knitters

You will notice that I often talk about the 'back', 'middle' or 'front' in relation to making a stitch. 'Front' is closest to you, 'back' is furthest away from you, and 'middle' is in between the two knitting needles when they are crossed over.

How to do knit stitch

Start with the needle with the cast-on stitches in your left hand and the empty needle in your right hand.

Step 1: Pick it up. Insert the tip of the right-hand needle into the stitch on the left-hand needle – from the bottom to the top. Keep the needles crossed, left over right.

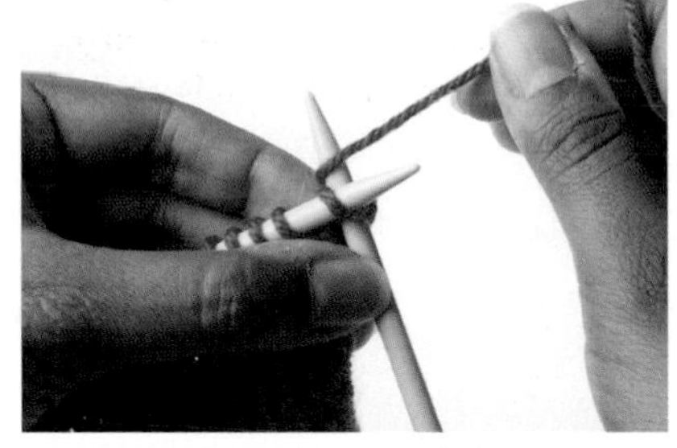

Step 2: Back and then middle. Holding both the needles in your left hand (between the thumb and first two fingers) wrap the long end of the yarn to the back of both needles (away from you) and then through the middle of the needles (back towards you).

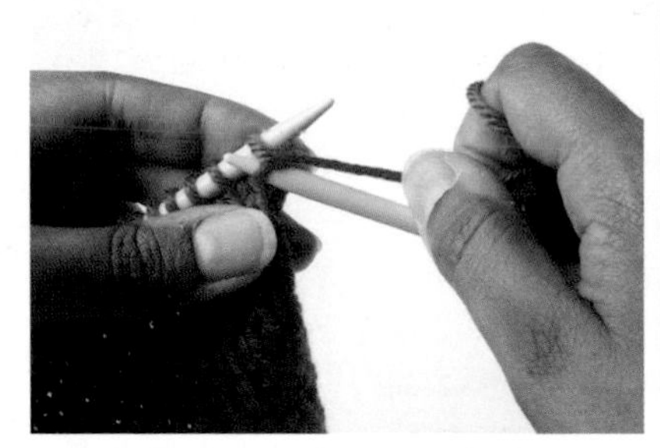

Step 3: Underneath and to the front. Bring the tip of the right-hand needle under the first loop on the left-hand needle.

Step 4: Release. Gently push the stitch on the left-hand needle off, using your left thumb. Repeat to the end of the row.

How to do purl stitch

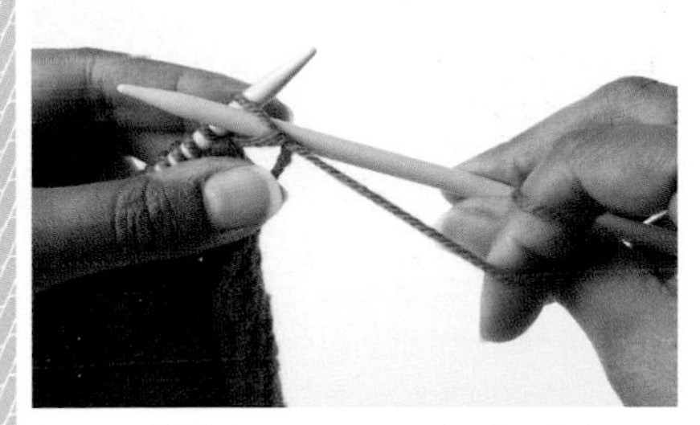

Step 1: Pick it up. Insert the tip of the right-hand needle into the stitch on the left-hand needle – from top to the bottom. Keep the needles crossed, right over left. The yarn should be at the front of the work.

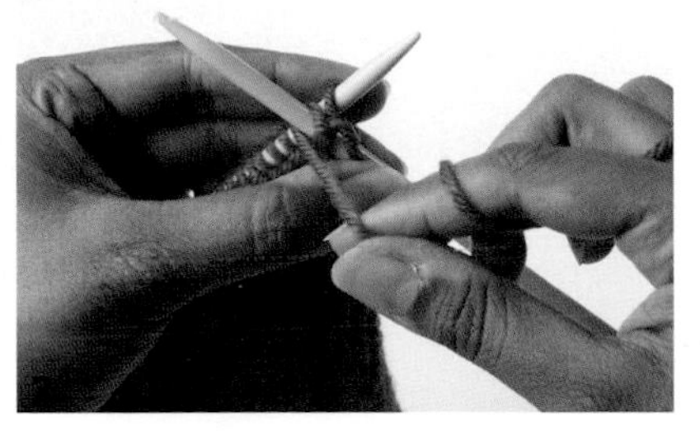

Step 2: Middle and then front. Holding both the needles in your left hand (between thumb and first two fingers), wrap the long end of the yarn through the middle of the needles and then to the front of the needles.

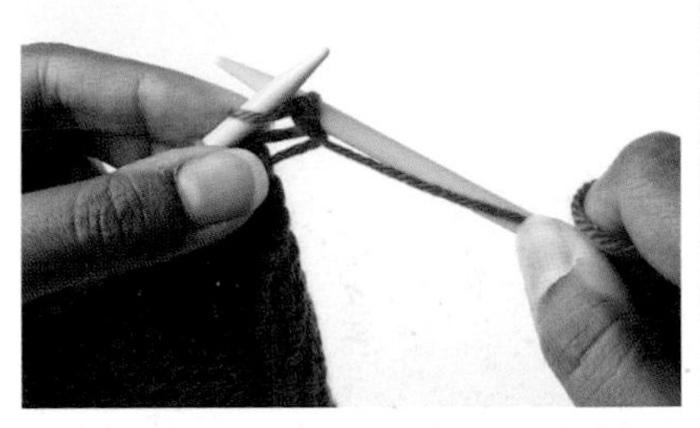

Step 3: Underneath and to the back. Take the tip of the right-hand needle under the first loop on the left-hand needle and to the back of the left-hand needle.

Step 4: Release. Gently push the stitch on the left-hand needle off, using your left thumb. Repeat to the end of the row.

Garter stitch = if you knit every row.

Stocking stitch = if you knit one row, then purl one row, and repeat.

Stitch combinations

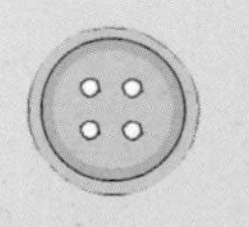

Handy HINT

Once you can knit and purl in combination, you have hundreds of stitches at your fingertips. Experiment, concentrate and don't forget to count your stitches at the end of every row.

Rib stitch. If you alternate knit and purl stitches on an even number of cast-on stitches, you get 1 x 1 rib.

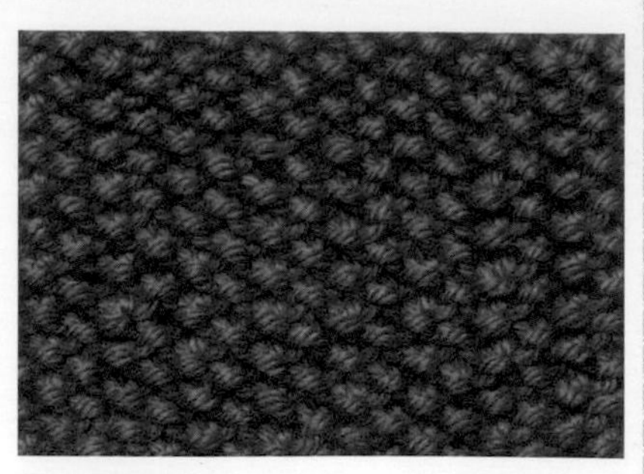

Moss stitch. If you alternate knit and purl stitches on an odd number of cast-on stitches, you get moss stitch.

Note to Knitters

When you knit, the right-hand needle goes to the back and the yarn is held to the back.

When you purl, the right-hand needle goes to the front and the yarn is held to the front.

When you work with knit and purl stitches, you have to move the yarn to the back, over and between the needles when you are knitting and to the front when you are purling. Pay attention, or you'll end up with a mistake!

Shaping: decreasing and increasing

Note to Knitters

Shaping knitting is essential if you want to do more than knit in straight lines. By learning how to increase and decrease, you can knit any shape you want and this will be invaluable if and when you choose to design your own knitting patterns, or adapt patterns to suit your shape.

Decreasing

There are lots of ways of doing everything in knitting. In my first book, which was for the absolute beginner to knitting, I only showed you one basic way of doing each technique. For example, decreasing was K2tog. Now I want to add to your shaping repertoire and abbreviation know-how.

How you choose to decrease will affect the finished look of your edging. There are different methods depending on which way your knitted edge will slant.

In this picture, the right-hand slope is slanting to the left and the left-hand slope is slanting to the right – this is with the right side of the work facing you (i.e. the knit side on stocking stitch). Please note that this is not a fully fashioned raglan, as the shaping is done right at the edge of the knitting. (A fully fashioned raglan is when the shaping is made one or two stitches in from the edge of the knitting so it shows as a ridge on the edge – you'll see this in the Ladies' raglan jumper on p.52.)

The simplest way of decreasing is K2tog or P2tog. Both these methods give you a slant to the right – as you look at the knitting from the right side of the work (on stocking stitch).

K2tog = Knit two stitches together.

P2tog = Purl two stitches together.

To create a left slant

On the knit side – this is the right side (RS) of the work – K2tog tbl. This means that you knit two stitches together through the back of the loops – pick up the stitches, wrap the yarn back and middle around the back needle, bring that needle underneath and to the front, and release both stitches.

On the purl side – this is the wrong side of the work (WS) – P2tog tbl. This means that you purl two stitches together through the back of the loops – bring the needle to the front, wrap the yarn middle and front around the front needle, bring that needle underneath and to the back, and release both stitches.

K2tog tbl

K2tog tbl = Knit two stitches together through the back of the loop.

P2tog tbl

P2tog tbl = Purl two stitches together through the back of the loops.

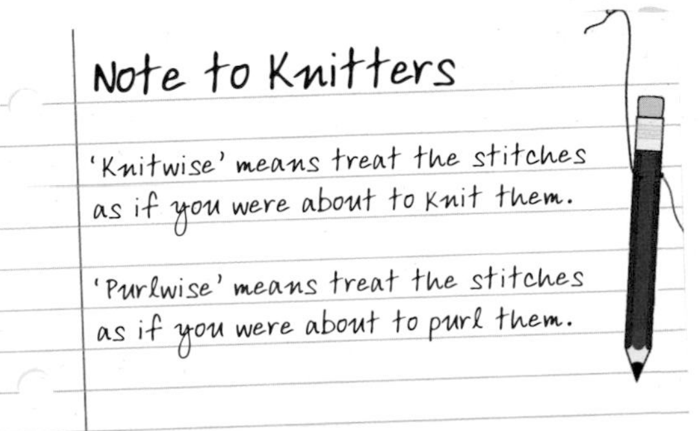

continue...

Decreasing *continued…*

SSK = Slip, Slip, Knit

Step 1: Slip two stitches, one by one, knitwise (as if you were about to knit them), from the left needle to the right needle, without knitting them.

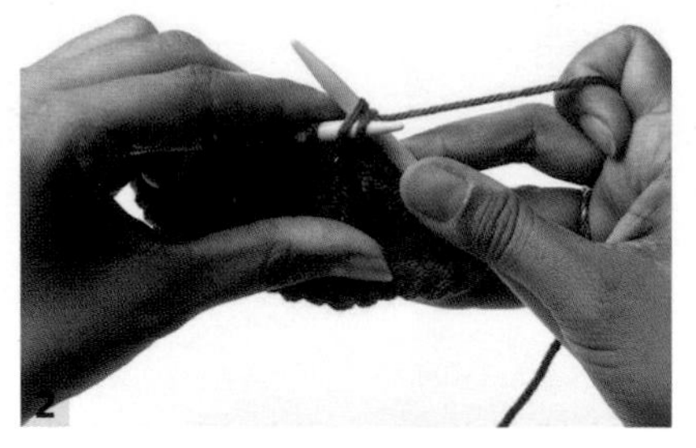

Step 2: Insert the left-hand needle into the front of both these stitches: you are now in position to knit the two stitches together.

Step 3: If you look closely at the base of the stitch you've knitted, you can see that it slants to the left. This will become more apparent the more decrease rows you knit.

SKP = Slip, Knit, Pass (or SKPO = Slip, Knit, Pass Over)

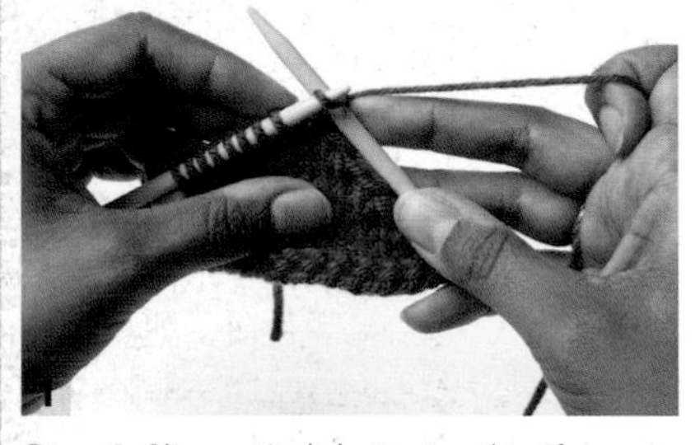

Step 1: Slip a stitch knitwise (as if you were about to knit it).

Step 2: Knit the next stitch.

Step 3: Pass the slipped stitch over the knitted stitch by inserting the left-hand needle down into the front of the slipped stitch on the right-hand needle, then lift it over the stitch you have just knitted (as if you were casting it off). There is now one less stitch remaining on the right-hand needle.

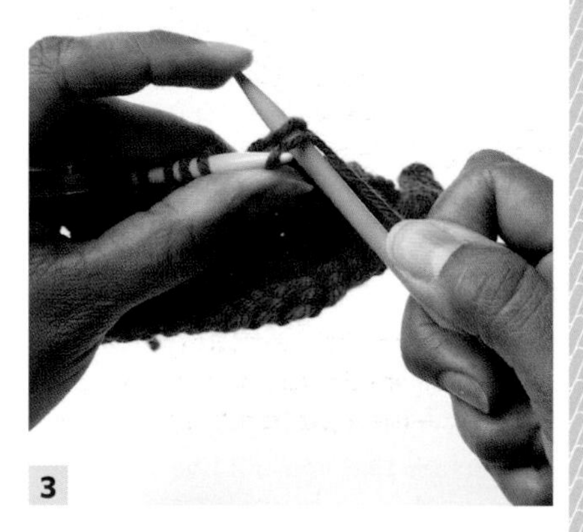

Increasing

M1 = Make One

The simplest way of increasing is M1 = Make one stitch. This is where you pick up the loop in between two stitches and knit it.

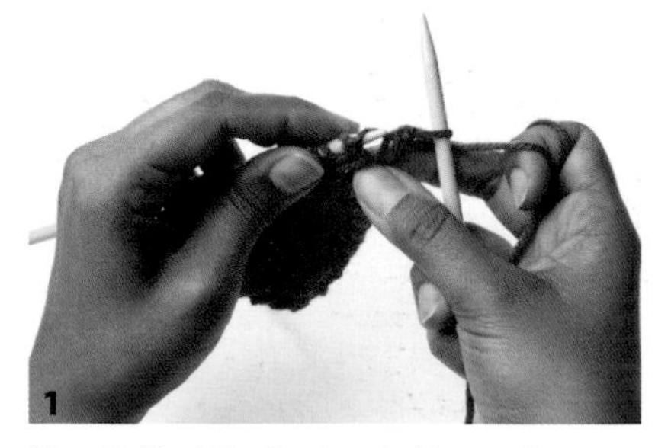

Step 1: Find the horizontal loop of yarn that runs between two stitches and pick it up towards you with the left-hand needle, from the back to the front.

Step 2: Then knit the loop that you have just picked up. It'll feel tight, but this is normal.

Note to Knitters

M1 on a purl row is just the same. Pick up the loop of yarn between two stitches, towards you, i.e. from the back to the front.

KFB = Knit Front and Back

Another way of increasing you'll often see in patterns is KFB. The result doesn't look very different from an increase made by M1, but it's still a useful trick to have up your knitted sleeve.

Step 1: Pick up the stitch, wrap the yarn around the needle, and work the stitch but do not release it from the left-hand needle.

Step 2: Then pick up the same stitch by going into the back of it.

Step 3: Wrap the yarn around the back needle, back and then middle.

Step 4: Work the stitch by bringing the right-hand needle under and to the front.

Step 5: Now release the stitch. You'll see that you have two stitches on the right-hand needle where you've knitted twice into one stitch, thus increasing!

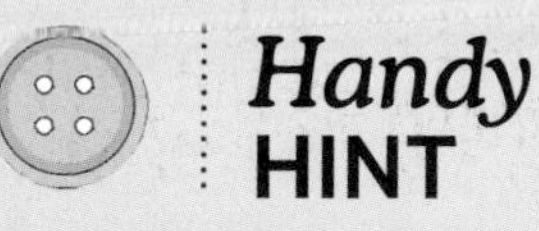

Rule number one:
It's very important that you always have the correct number of stitches, especially after a decrease or increase row. Count your stitches!

Casting off

Basic cast-off

Casting off (or binding off) is what you do when you have completed your knitting, so it can live independently from the needles. It's your first step in achieving a neat finish (this is something I'll talk about a lot in this book!).

Step 1: Knit two stitches.

Step 2: Insert the tip of the left-hand needle down into the first stitch that you knitted on the right-hand needle.

Step 3: Lift the lower stitch over the top stitch and off the right-hand needle. Finally, release the stitch you lifted over the right needle off the left needle. You will then have one stitch on the right-hand needle

Step 4: Keep casting off in the same way, until you have one stitch left on the right-hand needle and the left-hand needle is empty. Then cut the yarn, leaving a tail, which you will need to weave in later.

Step 5: Pass the cut end of the yarn through the last stitch left on the knitting needle, and pull it tight. This is called fastening off.

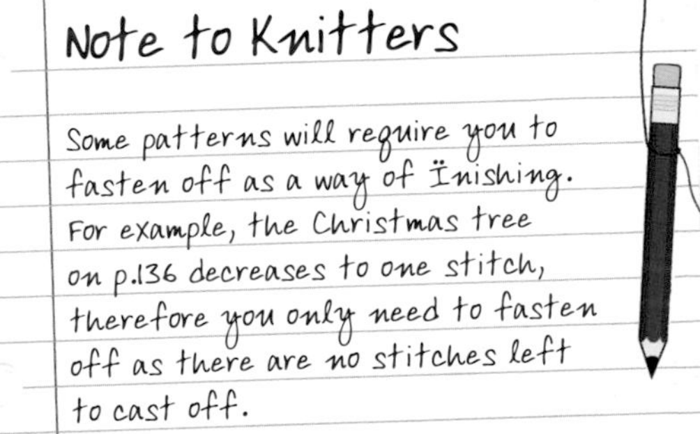

Note to Knitters

Some patterns will require you to fasten off as a way of ïnishing. For example, the Christmas tree on p.136 decreases to one stitch, therefore you only need to fasten off as there are no stitches left to cast off.

Drawstring finish

A drawstring finish is a way of finishing your knitting as an alternative to casting off. It works when you want the knitting to have a rounded edge, for example at the top of a hat or the fingers of gloves.

Step 1: Cut the yarn, leaving a long tail, and thread it onto a darning needle.

Step 2: Pass the darning needle through the stitches remaining on the knitting needle one by one, removing them off the knitting needle as they are secured by the yarn on the darning needle.

Step 3: Pull the yarn tightly: you'll see that it acts like a drawstring on the stitches. You can now use the yarn on the darning needle to sew up your seam as required in your pattern.

Three-needle bind-off

The three-needle bind-off is one of my all-time favourite techniques. It's a hugely satisfying way of finishing your work if you have two edges that need to be sewn together – for example on the top of a hood, as I'll show you in the Versatile kiddies' jumper pattern on p.72. I promise that once you've had a go, you won't tire of showing off the tidy finish on the outside and the inside of your work!

Step 1: You need to start with the same number of stitches on two needles. Hold both the needles in your left hand, with the right sides of the work facing each other and the points of the needles facing to the right. (If all your stitches are on one straight needle, transfer half your stitches onto another needle, with the points of both needles facing the edges of the knitted piece.)

Step 2: Using a third straight knitting needle, the same size as you've been knitting with, and held in your right hand, pick up a stitch from the tips of both needles, as if you were knitting (knitwise). First, you pick up the stitch from the needle closest to you, then from the needle that's further away from you.

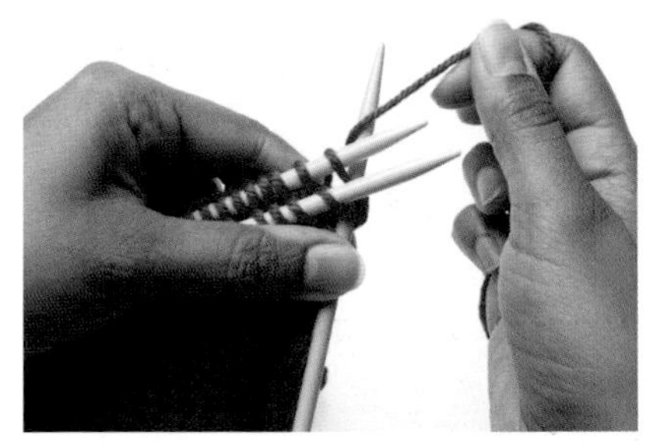

Step 3: When you have picked up these two stitches, knit them together (it's a bit fiddly, but persevere!).

You'll be releasing both the stitches on the left-hand needles at the same time as you knit them together. You will now have one stitch knitted on the right-hand needle.

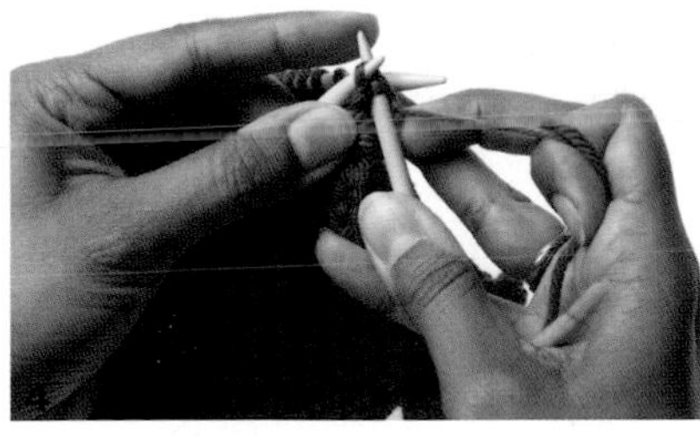

Step 4: Repeat so you have two stitches on the right-hand needle. Then, using the tip of the needle nearest to you in your left hand, lift the first stitch on the right-hand needle over the second stitch, thus casting it off.

Continue along the row. You are now casting off using three needles!

You'll see on the right side of the work that this gives you a really neat finish.

Continue casting off all the stitches in the same way to the end, then fasten off as normal. Weave the end of the yarn into the wrong-side seam of your cast-off. Turn your knitting the right side out and see your neat finish – you'll soon see why this is one of my favourite techniques!

Kitchener stitch

Kitchener stitch gives a similar-looking finish to a three-needle bind-off, but uses a different technique. You'll get a very tidy result, which is useful for finishing the toe of a sock, for example.

To set up, you need the same number of stitches on two needles. Hold the work with the right side facing outwards, and arrange your needles so that they are parallel to each other, and both tips are pointing towards the right. Hold the work in your left hand.

Cut the yarn, leaving a long tail, and thread it onto a darning needle – hold this in your right hand.

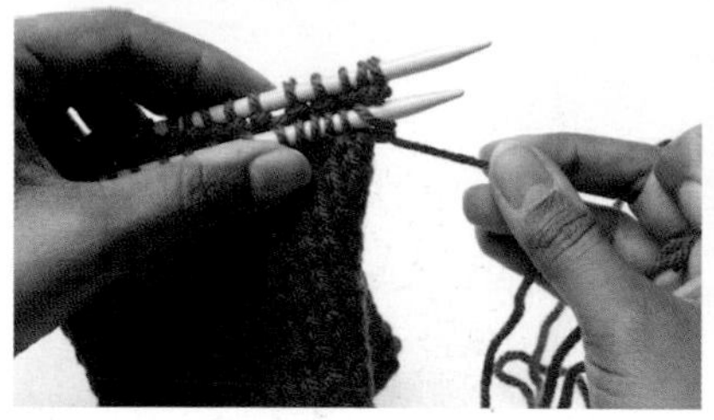

To start, insert the darning needle into the front stitch (the one on the knitting needle nearest to you) purlwise (as if to purl) and pull the yarn through.

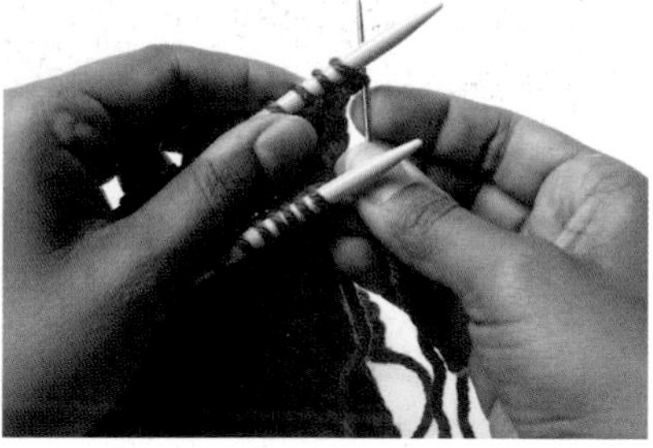

Then insert the darning needle into the back stitch (the one on the knitting needle furthest away from you) knitwise (as if to knit). Pull the yarn through the stitches, leaving the stitches on the knitting needle.

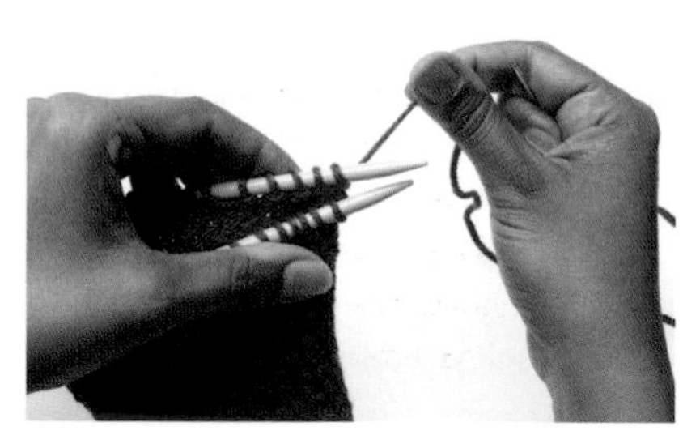

Please note that you only need to do this at the beginning of your Kitchener stitch.

Note to Knitters

Kitchener stitch is also sometimes called grafting.

Kitchener stitch: now repeat the following instructions until you have one stitch left on each knitting needle:

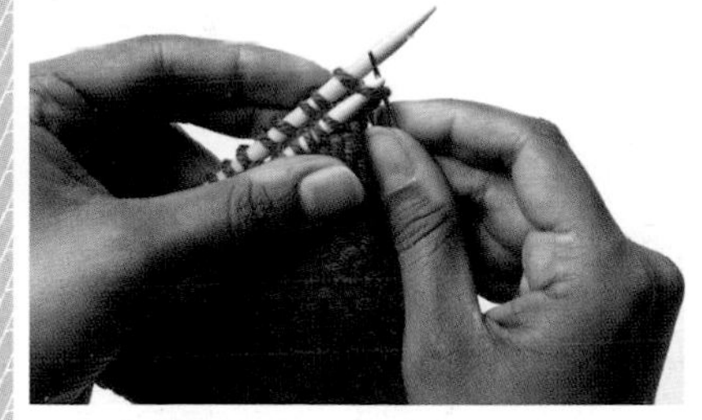

Step 1: Insert the darning needle into the front stitch knitwise, and slip the stitch off the knitting needle.

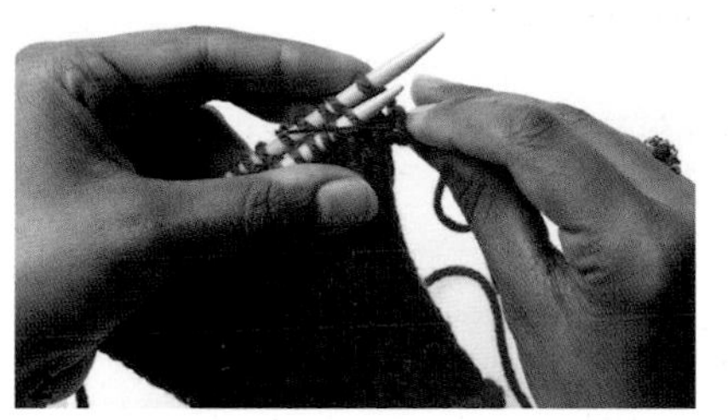

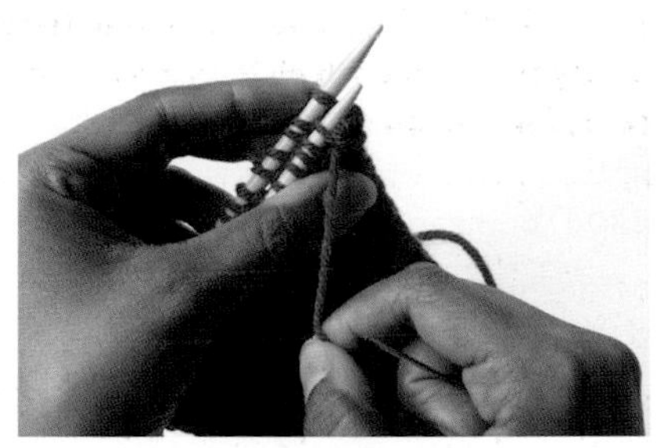

Step 2: Then insert the darning needle into the front stitch purlwise, leave the stitch on the knitting needle and pull the yarn through both stitches.

Step 3: Insert the darning needle into the back stitch purlwise, and slip the stitch off the knitting needle.

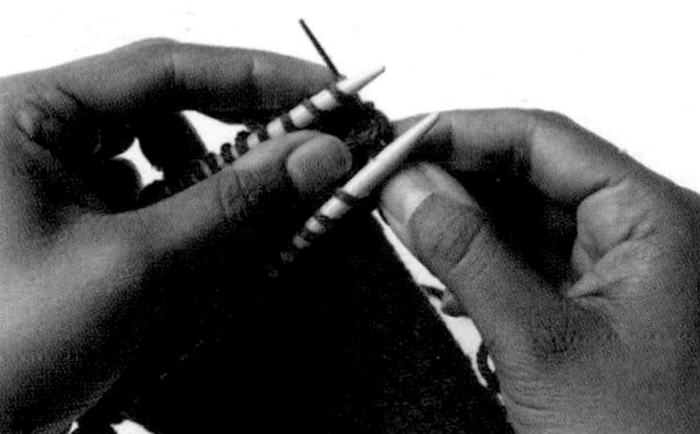

Step 4: Then push the darning needle into the back stitch knitwise, leave the stitch on the knitting needle and pull the yarn through both stitches.

Continue in this way – you'll soon see your tidy finish!

Repeat steps 1–4 until you have one stitch remaining on each of the needles in your left hand.

To finish the last two stitches, slip the front stitch knitwise and slip the back stitch purlwise. Pull the yarn through. Then take the yarn to the inside of the work by pushing the darning needle through to the inside of your sewn-up knitting.

Weave the end into the wrong side of your knitting and enjoy the tidy finish.

A little phrase that I repeat to myself as I do Kitchener stitch might help you:

Front: knit, slip, purl, leave – pull through.

Back: purl, slip, knit, leave – pull through.

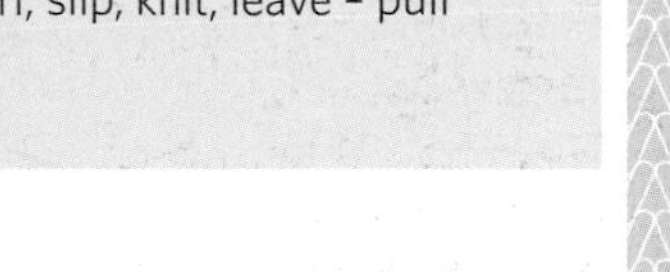

Finishing techniques

I-cord

I-cord is a method for knitting a very small tube. You use two double-pointed needles. This technique is a pretty cute way of finishing off a kiddy's hat (see p.106) or it can be used to knit limbs for your toys (see p.128).

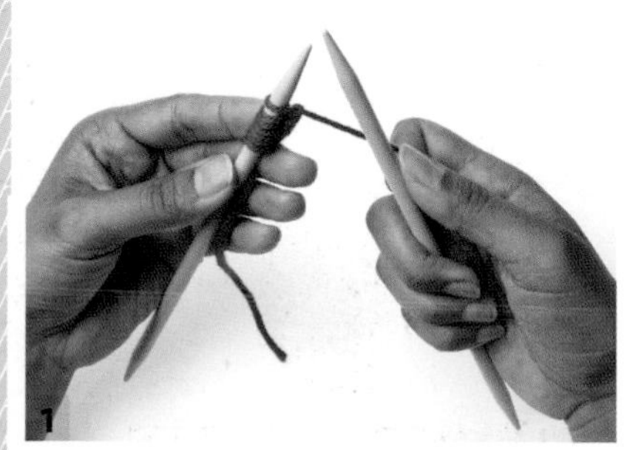

Step 1: Cast on the number of stitches your pattern requires onto a double-pointed needle (dpn).

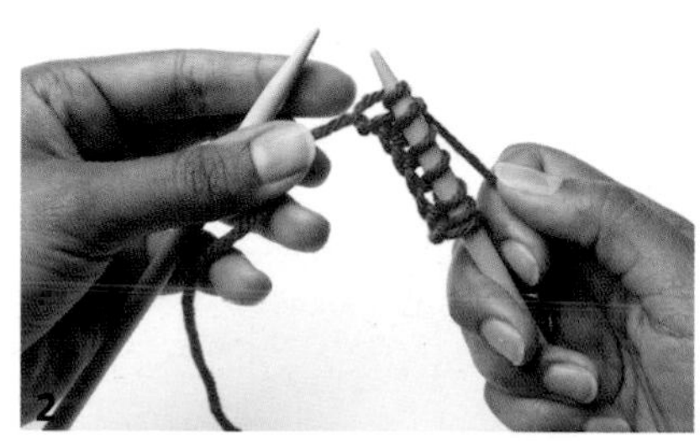

Step 2: Knit one row.

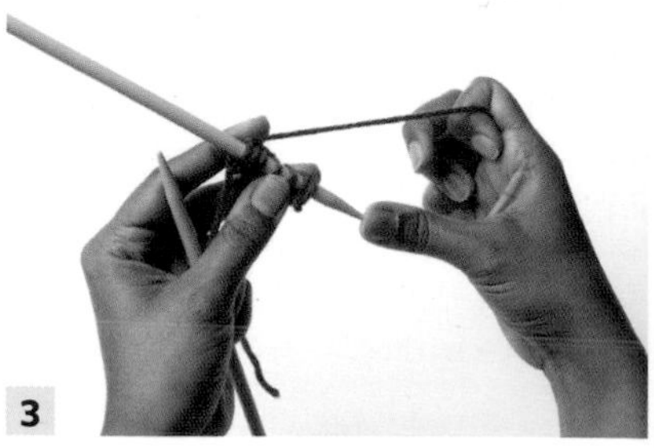

Step 3: Slide the knitting down to the other end of the double-pointed knitting needle.

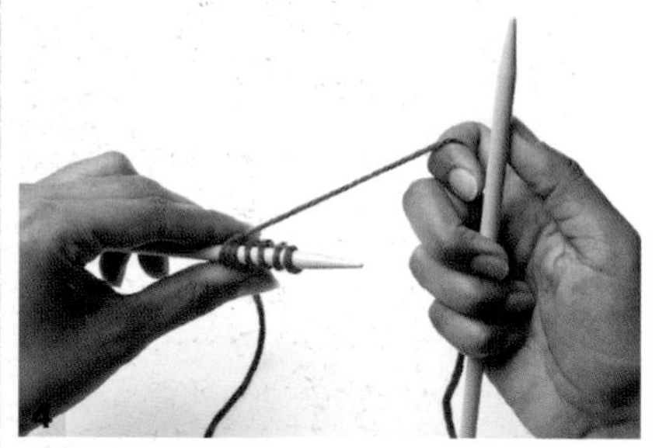

Step 4: Hold the knitting in your left hand and pull the yarn to the right.

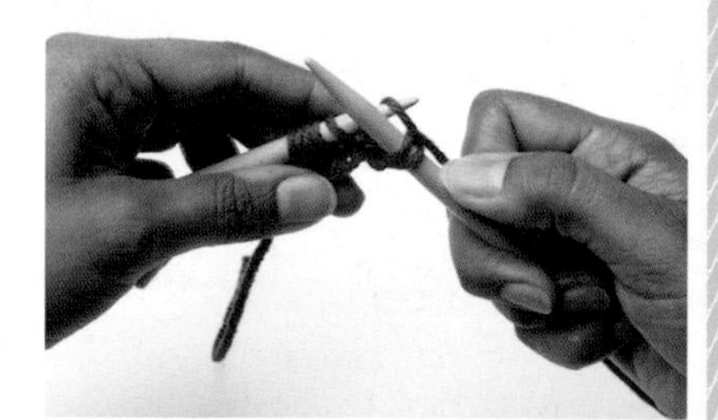

Step 5: Knit the next row with the yarn pulled from the other side of the knitting. This will feel strange, but you have to trust me here!

Continue in this way, every time sliding the stitches to the other end of the double-pointed needle and knitting the next row by pulling the yarn to the right.

At the end of every few rows, pull the knitting down from the needle to stretch it a bit. You'll soon see your I-cord forming.

To finish, you can cast off normally or use a drawstring finish and weave the end into the inside of your I-cord.

Pick up and knit

This is a technique whereby you pick up stitches from one edge of a piece of knitting and continue working in that direction. You'll mostly see it used for neckbands on sweaters and button bands on cardigans. I love it, as it makes for such a neat finish. You'll need a crochet hook to pick up the stitches – use one in a size close to, or slightly smaller than that of the knitting needles.

Step 1: Lay out your work with the right side facing upwards. You will be picking up the stitches from the right to the left of the knitting, and not from left to right as you might imagine it to be done. Insert the crochet hook into the edge of the work, making sure that it slides under two loops of yarn.

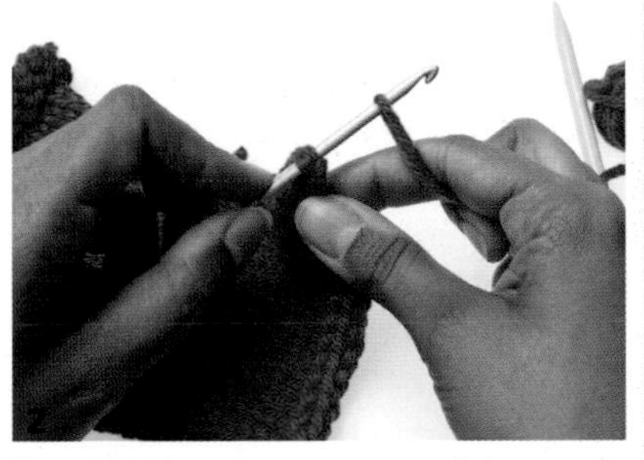

Step 2: Wrap the yarn around the crochet hook and pull the hook back out from the two loops of yarn.

Step 3: Place this yarn on a knitting needle (which will be pointing to the left).

Continue picking up stitches along the edge of your knitting in this way.

When picking up stitches from a long length of knitting, I suggest that you mark out sections with dressmaking pins. Divide each section into eight equal parts and work out how many stitches you need to pick up per section. This will ensure that you don't get to the end and discover that you are way out on your numbers.

Buttonholes

You can knit a small buttonhole by following this basic instruction: YF, K2tog (yarn forward, knit two together). The size of your buttonhole will be relative to your yarn and needle size.

Buttonholes are often worked on a ribbed border; the technique for working buttonholes is the same, whatever stitch you are using, but I'll be showing it to you on a rib as it's a useful bit of knowledge to have.

Note to Knitters

Knitting with the yarn forward gives you an extra stitch, and knitting two stitches together gives you one fewer stitch, so you'll have the same number of stitches at the end of the row as you started with.

continue...

Buttonholes in a ribbed border

To get a really tidy finish for buttonholes on a ribbed border, you need to know exactly when to rib. A pattern will often tell you to rib a certain number of stitches in between the buttonholes. To do this, you need to be able to tell whether the next stitch is a knit or a purl simply by looking at it. For a refresher on this, see Recognising rib stitches (p.40).

For example, the pattern could say: '[rib 12, YF, K2tog], repeat a further ten times'. To rib 12, you need to know exactly which stitch to start ribbing with: a knit or a purl. So you would work 12 stitches of rib (starting with a knit or a purl as the pattern demands), then YF, K2tog – that sequence of knitting will give you a buttonhole with 12 stitches of rib in between each buttonhole.

Note to Knitters

I can't tell you how useful it is to know by looking if a stitch is a knit stitch (a V-shape) and which is a purl stitch (a wave or a shallow U-shape). Take time to understand the structure of stitches and you'll become a more accomplished and conïdent knitter.

Step 1: Work to where you want the buttonhole to be.

Step 2: YF (bring the yarn to the front of the work, in between the two needles).

Step 3: K2tog (knit the next two stitches together).

Make sure, at the end of the buttonhole row, that you have the same number of stitches as you started with.

In the row after the buttonhole row, you'll continue your rib as you have been doing in previous rows (continue as 'set'). When you get to where you made a buttonhole, it will look a bit like a crossed-over stitch. This isn't a mistake – this is how it should look after you've worked the YF, K2tog.

Continue ribbing over the buttonhole stitch, making sure to follow your stitches accurately.

At the end of the row after the buttonhole row, you should see the buttonholes appear neatly!

Blocking

Blocking is a technique by which you stretch and shape a knitted fabric into specific dimensions. This can be helpful if your work needs to be a certain shape, or if two knitted pieces need to be exactly the same size, or if the holes in lace knitting need to be more opened up to show off the pattern.

This is a tricky subject for me, as my personal opinion conflicts with the traditional view. The traditional view is that all knitting should be blocked if you want to achieve a good finish. Personally, however, I don't always like the look of blocked knitting, as I feel it flattens the texture of the fabric and, for me, spoils the natural look of knitting. This is especially true on raised stitches such as cable work.

However, I do approve of blocking for fine lace patterns. Lacework on delicate yarn does benefit from blocking, as it opens out the weave of the fabric and shows it to its best advantage. I also use blocking on 'whimsies' such as the knitted Christmas tree (see p.136), as it helps to stiffen the shape.

If you find that a garment you've knitted is coming out a bit smaller than you expected, blocking can put some ease into the fabric, therefore making it a little bigger. But beware, as this isn't an exact science!

Techniques

There are several techniques for blocking:

1. Pin and spray (shown below).

2. Steam blocking. This is where you pin the garment to an ironing board and hold a steam iron over it, very close to the surface but not quite touching, and then press the steam button. Do this all over the fabric, wait a couple of hours until the fabric is completely dry and then unpin it. Repeat a couple of times before unpinning for very fine lace: see the Fir tree lace shawl on p.158.

3. Wet blocking. This is the most drastic method of blocking, which I suggest you use only on very fine lacework. Immerse the knitting in cool water (beware of using water that's too warm, especially with wool fibres). Lay out a sheet of plastic (a bin bag will do) and cover it with towels larger than the piece of knitting. Lay the wet knitting on the towels and pin the work into the shape and dimensions you want it to be. Then you can remove any excess moisture by laying more towels on top of the work and pressing gently. Leave the work pinned in position until it's completely dry.

4. Weight blocking. This is where you spray the knitting, cover it and weigh it down with heavy books until it is dry. This will stiffen the knitting into shape. See the Christmas tree on p.136.

The pin and spray method

You can see on these squares of Fir tree lace (see p.158), that the square on the left has been blocked and the square on the right has not.

Step 1: Pin the piece into shape on a padded surface (for example an ironing board, a large piece of foam or a specialised knitting board). Your pattern may specify dimensions for the knitted fabric; if so, follow these.

Step 2: Spray the fabric with a mist of water and leave until dry.

Sewing up

For most knitters, sewing up isn't their favourite part of a knitting project. In fact, I know lots of knitters who knit in the round in order to avoid it as much as they can. But I'm different – I really enjoy finishing a project and getting it to look as professional as possible, because it doesn't matter how good a knitter you are, if you bodge something together, it will show!

The tricksy thing about sewing up is that it's a little bit different every time, depending on the stitch you're knitting with and the angle of the edge of your work. I'll try and show you a few different ways of sewing up to add to your repertoire and help you to take a big step towards making your knitting neat and professional, with a touch of class.

Note to Knitters

I've used a contrasting coloured yarn for sewing up to make it clearer on the photos, but you should of course use the same yarn you've been knitting with. Sorry if this is stating the obvious, but there's always one...!

Mattress stitch

This stitch will give you an invisible finish if both the pieces to be joined are knitted in stocking stitch (knit one row, purl one row). It can also be used when working with rib stitch.

These two pieces of stocking stitch knitting are side by side

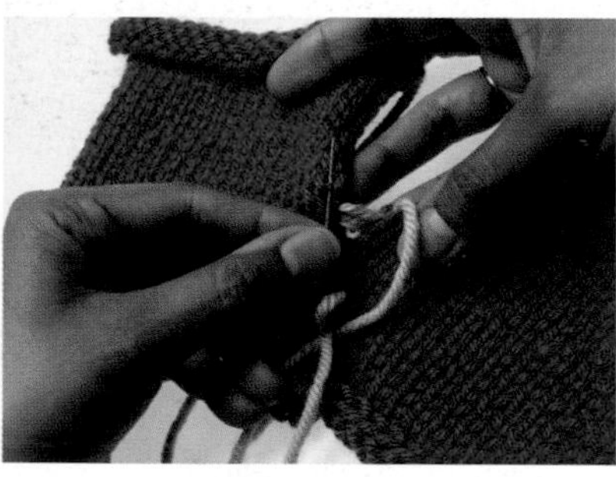

If you look closely at the 'V' of the stitch and dig your darning needle into the 'V', you'll pick up a horizontal bar inside the 'V'.

Pick up the centre bar from one side, then the next and so on, back and forth. After you've picked up about four centre bars, pull tight and you'll see that you've sewn up the pieces with a near-invisible finish. You'll often be using the centre-bar technique for the side and underarm seams of your cardigans and jumpers.

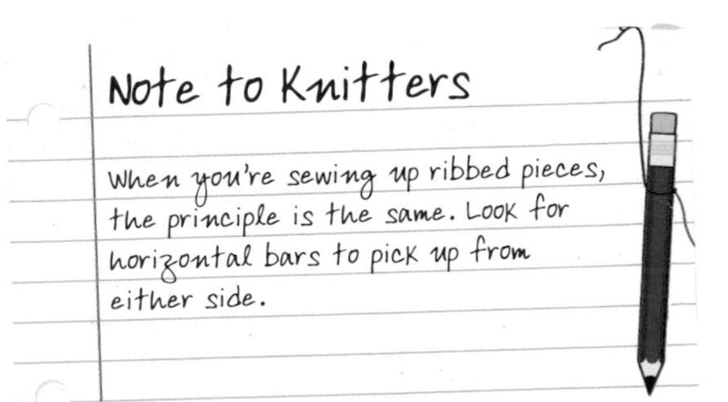

These two pieces of stocking stitch knitting are end to end

If your pieces of knitting are end to end, for example a shoulder seam, you need to pick up the two sides of the 'V' of the stitch with your darning needle.

Pick up the two 'V' sides from one piece, then the other, about four times before pulling tight for a neat finish.

If you feel like you aren't getting a tidy finish, try again; this time working a little further in from the very edge of your knitted piece. You'll find it isn't as neat if you're trying to find your centre bars and sides of the 'V' too near the edge of the knitting.

These two pieces of stocking stitch knitting have the end and side facing each other

This situation might occur when you are sewing a sleeve into the body of a jumper or cardigan.

If your pieces of knitting face in different directions, as they would if you were sewing a sleeve into the body of a garment, for example, you mix both techniques. On one side, pick up the centre bar, and on the other side, pick up two sides of the 'V'. Pull tight for a neat finish.

Sewing a sleeve into a body

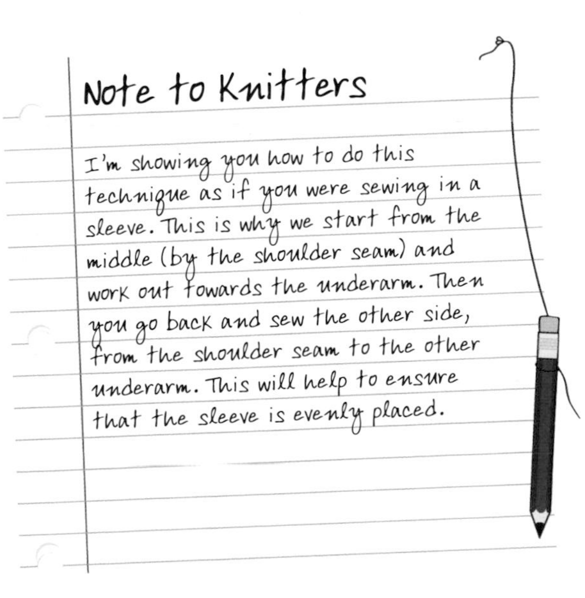

The sleeve is on the right and the body piece with the shoulder seam is on the left. Start sewing up in the centre, by the shoulder seam. Note that you are picking up the centre bar on the body (on the left) and two sides of the 'V' on the sleeve (on the right).

continue...

Sewing a sleeve into a body *continued...*

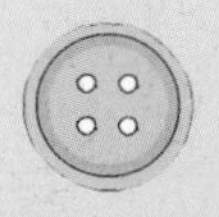

Handy HINT

Thread a darning needle with a long piece of yarn when you start sewing in the middle. When you pull the yarn through the first stitch, leave a long enough tail for you to go back and sew the other half of the sleeve with the same piece of yarn.

Here's what the final seam should look like. Another nice, neat finish!

Angled edges (not fully fashioned)

These two pieces of knitting have an angled edge – this could be some shaping around a sleeve or a (not fully fashioned) raglan edge. You can see that I'm picking up the centre bar from each side, then pulling the yarn tight for a tidy finish.

You can see here the finish you'll get if you are sewing up a raglan that is not fully fashioned – this is where the decreases are made right at the edge of the knitting. You'll be using this technique on sections of the Ladies' classic cardigan on p.80.

Angled edges (fully fashioned)

Look out for this technique on the Ladies' raglan jumper on p.52.

You can see that the decreases are more defined on this piece of knitting, as they are made one stitch in from the edge: K1, SSK, K to last 3sts, K2tog, K1.

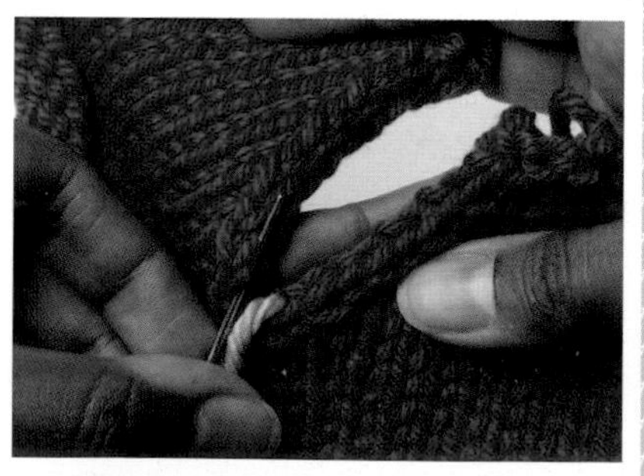

Once again, you are picking up the centre bar from each side, but you are leaving one fully distinct stitch on the inside of the work. You can see it clearly on the left of the darning needle.

When you pull up the yarn tightly, you'll see one stitch at the edge of the raglan on each side. These come together to make two neat stitches, side by side along the sewn seam.

Here's your tidy finish!

The principle is the same on a fully fashioned finish where the decreases are made two stitches in from the edge, for example in the Men's bulky jumper on p.60.

Sewing up around corners

Here I'm sewing in a right-angled piece (see, for example, the modified drop shoulder in the Versatile kiddies' jumper on p.72). I mix and match my centre bar and two sides of the 'V' techniques as I need to.

You can see that the result took plenty of initiative, but it's worth it for the final look.

These angles are as you might find when sewing up a fitted sleeve, as in the Ladies' classic cardigan (see p.80). I start off with two sides of the 'V' on both pieces.

Pull tight as you go.

What you'll find, as you gain experience in sewing up pieces with different angles, is that you'll have to adjust your sewing from one side to the next. Don't be afraid to undo a few stitches and try them another way until you get a satisfying finish.

Sewing up garter stitch

Look closely at the garter stitch and you'll see ridges. Each ridge has a top and a bottom. With a darning needle and yarn, pick up the bottom ridge on one side.

Then pick up the top ridge on the other side, and work back and forth.

Pull the yarn tight every few stitches.

Whip stitch

This is a very simple stitch for sewing up, in which you pick up a loop from each side of the knitting.

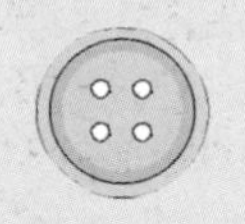

Handy HINT

You won't be tying knots at the beginning and end of your sewing up. Leave a long tail at each end and weave them in along the seam on the inside of your knitting.

Note to Knitters

You'll hear me go on and on about a tidy finish ... I don't want you to spend months knitting something and let yourself down with the sewing up. Be patient and it'll be worth it in the end!

Easing in

Handy **HINT**

As well as paying attention to the spot you are sewing, also remember to keep an eye on the end point – that's the point in the knitting where the sewing-up should end neatly.

This is a technique that you might know if you sew, but it's just as useful for a knitter when making up projects and garments. Sometimes the two pieces of knitted fabric you are sewing together won't be exactly the same length, row for row or stitch for stitch. This is often the case with sleeves, for example. This is when you have to 'ease in' your sewing or, as I call it, 'make it fit'. To make the two sides fit each other, every now and again, at regular intervals, you will need to pick up an extra loop of the fabric on the side that is longer.

If the centre-bar side is too long, occasionally (and evenly spread out throughout the length of the sewing-up), pick up two centre bars at once.

If the two sides of the 'V' side is too long, occasionally (and evenly spread out throughout the length of the sewing-up), pick up three 'V' sides at once.

Note to Knitters

You won't need to ease in if you are sewing up two pieces that are the same, for example, the front and back of the body part of a jumper, but it's still very useful to keep checking the end point of your sewing so that you can make sure the pieces will sew together accurately. If you find yourself a stitch or two out, you can use the trick of picking up an extra loop on the side that is longer.

Knitting SOS!

This chapter gives you some handy hints and tips to smooth your knitting journey, and also answers a few niggling questions that never seem to be explained in patterns. It's not an exhaustive list by any means, but is hopefully somewhere for you to turn in those head-scratching moments that all knitters have.

Knitting rules

Here are a few rules to make your knitting journey a smooth one. As you move on to more involved patterns and challenging techniques, I think you'll find them helpful for keeping your stitches in order.

Rule number one: At the end of every row, count your stitches! There's no getting away from this essential rule of knitting.

Rule number two: Never put down your knitting in the middle of a row. It's easy to lose concentration if you do, and you may make a mistake that could be hard to fix.

Rule number three: Try to knit at least two rows every day. You want to keep in the swing of knitting – leaving it for days (or worse still, weeks) at a time will make it less easy in the long run. This is especially true if you are working on a more complicated stitch or pattern.

Rule number four: This might seem to be a funny one, but you'll learn that it's essential! When knitting in a group with other knitters or crafters (and this is something I've learnt from experience with knitting students), always do your counting silently. There will always be someone else in the room who is counting at the same time, and we all know how annoying it is to lose count!

Handy HINT

Sometimes you will find that you run into something that just doesn't make sense, no matter how many times you try it. I still find this when writing a pattern or working out a new stitch. My tried and tested advice is to keep calm, take a break and come back to it later. There's really no point in flogging yourself when you are tired. I've often found that something I can't get right for hours in the evening can make sense in ten minutes when I'm fresh in the morning. I say again and again that knitting is about the journey as much as the destination.

Frogging: *how to un-knit your knitting*

We're all human ... even the perfectionists! Sometimes even the best knitters in the world will lose concentration and make a mistake. I reckon we all know what it's like to knit when we should have purled! So although I'm an advocate of the 'Keep Calm and Carry On' method of knitting, on occasion you will want or need to undo several stitches or rows.

Undoing your knitting one stitch at a time

This is for when you've made a mistake in a row so just need to backtrack for a few stitches.

In this image you can see that point A is the stitch that is currently on the needle. The hole at point B is the stitch below, which the current stitch is coming out of – this is the previous row to the row on the needle.

Insert the tip of the left needle, away from you, into the previous row.

Then push the stitch from the current row off the right-hand needle. Pull the end of the yarn - this will undo the stitch.

You can continue un-knitting one stitch at a time until you get to the place in your knitting before the mistake. Then, you'll find that you are already in the correct position to keep on knitting - with the knitted stitches on the right-hand needle and the stitches you've undone (to be knitted) on the left-hand needle.

Undoing several rows at a time

This is for use when you're really unhappy with what you've knitted and need to go back several rows. This is also known as 'frogging'.

Pull the stitches off the knitting needle (this can take guts) - but if it has to be done, then be brave! Pull on the yarn to unravel the knitting until you are at the row before the row you want to keep. You will undo this row, one stitch at a time, to get to the row you want to keep and put the stitches back on the knitting needle.

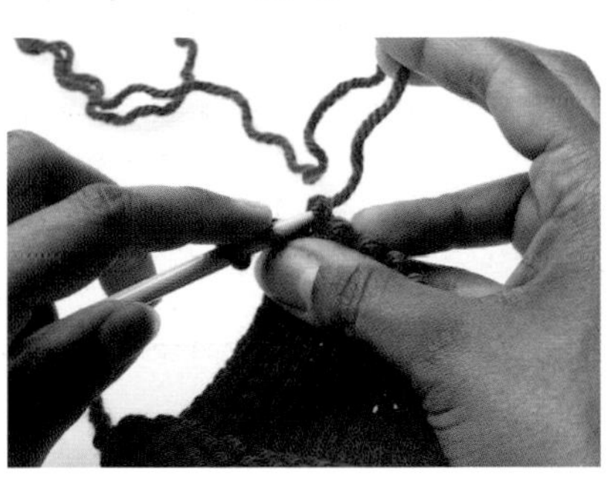

Hold the knitting in your right hand and the empty needle in your left hand. Put your thumb at the base of the first stitch, holding it firmly - this is to stop the stitch laddering any further than you want it to.

Gently pull the yarn out so that you are undoing only the first stitch on your work and follow through by simultaneously pushing the empty needle through the stitch, remembering to push the needle away from you.

On the needle in your left hand, you now have the first stitch of the row you want to start working from. Continue undoing the stitches one at a time and putting them safely back onto the left needle.

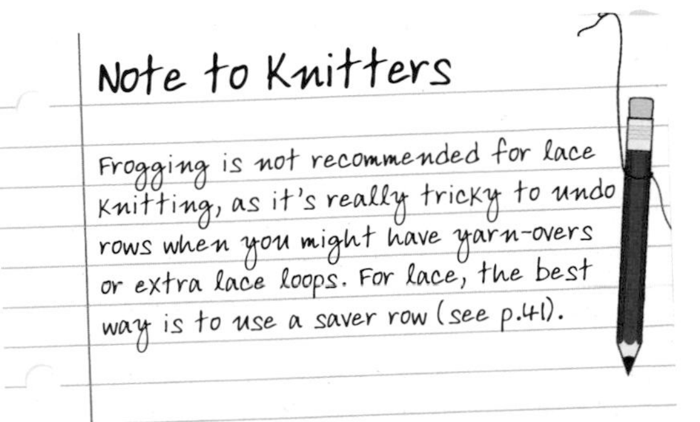

At this point, Rule number one is invaluable in helping you check that you picked up all the stitches. Count, count, count!

continue...

Frogging *continued…*

What NOT to do!

It's easy to make a mistake when picking up frogged stitches. You may think that you got it right, but then the next row will be very tight to knit and later on you'll see a row that looks a bit odd.

Here you can see a row where the stitches all look twisted. This is because the stitches have been put back on the knitting needle backwards.

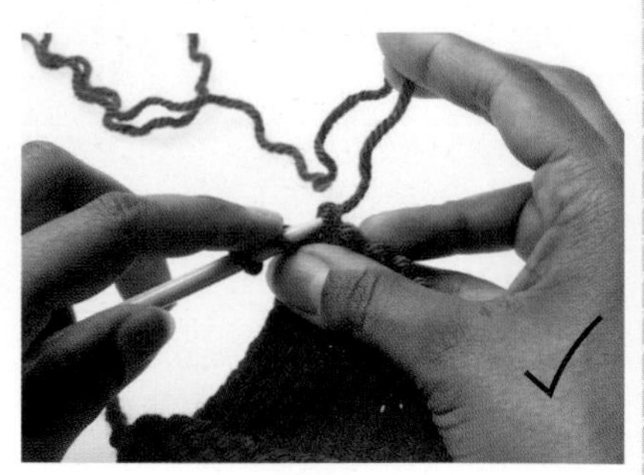

When you put the stitches back on the knitting needle, be sure to push the needle into the stitch AWAY FROM YOU.

If you put the needle through the stitch towards you, you've made a mistake. You'll notice this when you're knitting the next row, as it will feel really tight to knit.

Note to Knitters

Whether you are un-knitting knit or purl stitches, the principle is the same. If you can't easily find the previous row, try moving the yarn forwards or backwards between the needles, as this should make it clearer. And always push the needle away from you into the stitch.

Recognising rib stitches

Rib is where you knit and purl stitches so they appear in columns in your knitting. You'll mostly find ribbing on the cuffs and collars of jumpers and cardigans, and the cuffs of gloves and socks. It creates a stretchier fabric than garter or stocking stitch.

When you knit a stitch, the yarn is at the back.

When you purl a stitch, the yarn is at the front.

A very useful little trick is knowing exactly where you are on a rib row without having to count from the beginning of the row. If you know exactly what knit and purl stitches look like, you'll save a great deal of time and you'll have taken another step in really understanding the structure of your knitting, which will make you a more confident knitter.

Handy HINT

I like to describe my stitches as if they were little faces – with the stitch on the needle as the face. You can see that the first 'face' on the left-hand needle is wearing a V-neck jumper, and the stitch to its left is wearing a horizontal line that I call a polo-neck jumper. So you can remember this as: 'P' for polo, 'P' for purl. It may seem funny, but I guarantee that you'll be looking for the V-necks and polo-necks as an easy way of knowing which stitch you are on in a rib pattern!

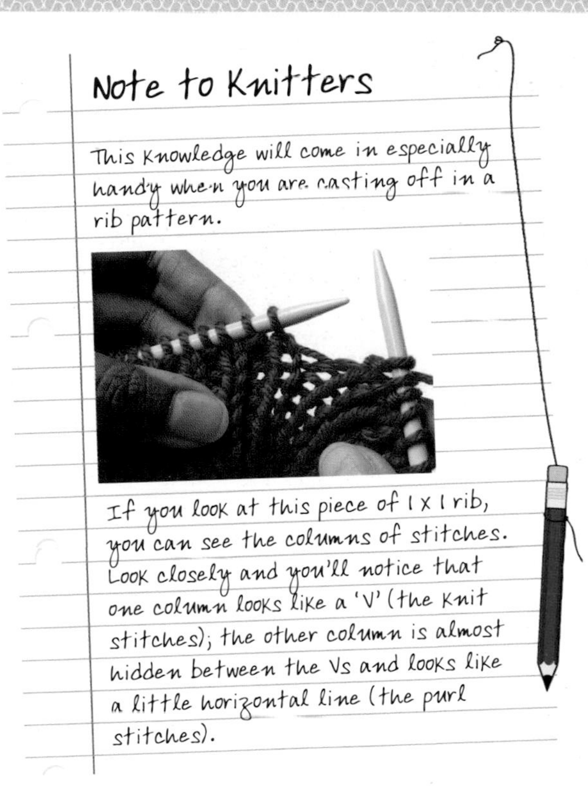

Saver row

Learning new stitches and knitting lace can be complicated, and a small lapse in concentration can mean you have the wrong number of stitches at the end of your row. Rather than having to undo an entire row, here's a little SOS trick to 'save' your stitches. I'm not a natural lace knitter, but love the effect of lace, so I found this technique really useful when knitting my Fir tree lace (see p.158). You can use this technique on any stitch pattern you like, if you're worried about going wrong.

Take a contrasting coloured yarn (cut a piece that is about three times the width of your knitting) and thread it onto a darning needle. When you are at the end of a repeat for a stitch pattern (about to start Row 1 of a stitch pattern sequence), thread the yarn through all the stitches on the knitting needle.

Thread the contrasting yarn through a couple of stitches at a time, and pull it through as you go, leaving a long tail dangling at each end.

You'll end up with a length of contrasting yarn running through all the stitches on the needle.

continue…

Saver row *continued…*

Continue knitting the pattern.

Note to Knitters

Only use a piece of saving yarn after the end of a pattern repeat. This way, you know that if you ever have to undo, you will start knitting again from Row 1 of your repeat.

If you make a mistake, simply pull out the knitting needle and undo the knitting until you get to the row that's on the saver yarn.

You'll see that the stitches won't undo any further than your saver row.

Then you'll easily be able to insert the knitting needle back into the stitches. Make sure you keep the working end of the yarn towards the tip of the knitting needle.

You are now ready to start knitting from Row 1 of the pattern repeat. The saver yarn can be pulled out whenever you want to remove it.

Note to Knitters

This SOS technique will work on all stitches – try it any time you are working on something new and are worried that you might make a mistake.

Turning

A pattern will sometimes instruct you to 'turn' the work in the middle of a row. Turning is what you do at the end of every row you knit, in order to be able to start the next row. It may seem counter-intuitive to turn in the middle of a row, but it will be for a good reason, so trust your pattern.

Here, I've turned in the middle of the row and am now ready to start working in the opposite direction.

Adding yarn

You can add new yarn at the end of a row, but it may be neater to add it in the middle of a row. The technique is the same either way.

When you are ready to add new yarn, tie the new end of the yarn around the end that's currently attached to the work (the end that is running out).

Push the knot of the new yarn down to the needle and simply continue knitting.

Weaving in ends

It's really important to give plenty of time and care to weaving in your ends of yarn. As with all aspects of 'finishing' your work, it'll make all the difference to the final knitted product. You can weave in ends with a crochet hook, but if you leave slightly longer ends, you can get a really tidy finish with a darning needle.

If you've added new yarn in the middle of a row, you'll spot a little hole where you changed yarn. Turn to the wrong side of the knitting and undo the little knot that was holding the new yarn in place.

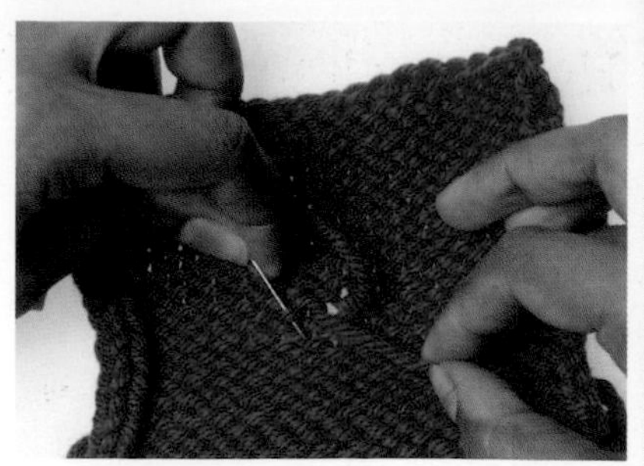

On the wrong side of the knitting, thread one of the ends through a darning needle. Then weave it in and out of the stitches, first taking the yarn over to the opposite side of the hole.

This crossing-over-the-hole technique makes sure that the hole vanishes neatly.

Weave the end up and down the stitches at the back of the work approximately five times. Pull the yarn

so that it is snug, but take care not to yank it too tightly or it will show on the front of the knitting.

Snip the ends close to the knitting once they have each been woven in about five times on each side.

You can see that the hole is now neatly closed up.

Note to Knitters

If you've added yarn at the end of a row, or have loose ends from sewing up, weave these ends in along the nearest seam. It's very like whip stitch (see p.36) – you are simply sewing in the ends about Ïve times so they are held securely without needing a knot.

Note to Knitters

If you'd prefer to add new yarn at the end of a row rather than in the middle, and when you have loose ends from sewing up, you can use a darning needle or crochet hook to weave ends in along a seam.

How to tell the right side from the wrong side

A pattern will often indicate whether you are knitting on the right side or wrong side of the work. This is usually just for your information. You don't have to do anything except make sure you are on the correct side of your knitting.

RS = Right side. On stocking stitch, the RS is the knit side.

WS = Wrong side. On stocking stitch, the WS is the purl side.

Working a two-row colour change

If you'd like to change the colours of your yarn in short bursts, here's how to do it without leaving hundreds of ends to weave in. This technique only works if you change colour every two rows, and use only two colours in your knitting.

This simple technique for working with two-row stripes can quickly transform any of the basic patterns in this book into something more colourful. I think it's especially effective to knit long, vertical stripes like those on the scarf on long circular needles (see p.121).

This works well on both stocking and garter stitch. The technique is the same on both. I've used it here on garter stitch to create a fine blue and pink striped pattern.

When you are ready to start your two-row stripe, join in the second colour (the blue in these photos) WITHOUT cutting off the first colour (the pink).

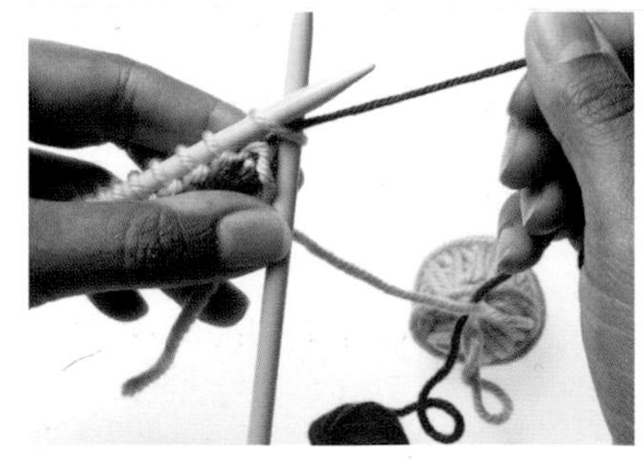

Work two rows using the second colour (knit two rows if you are using garter stitch; or knit one row, purl one row if you are using stocking stitch).

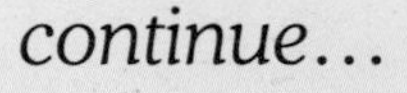

continue...

Working a two-row colour change *continued…*

Once you've worked these two rows, you'll find yourself back on the side of the knitting where you initially joined the second colour of yarn. Let go of the end of the second colour (blue), pick up the first colour (pink) and work two rows. The pink yarn will be carried up the side of the work to where you want to start knitting with it. The blue can simply wait at that end until you've worked two rows and are back at the end with the blue.

When you have worked two rows using the pink, you'll be back to the end with the blue yarn and can work the next two rows in blue.

Continue in this way, alternating two rows of each colour. The yarn not currently in use waits at the edge of the work, and the yarn in use is worked for two rows at a time. The yarn is carried up the side of the work and makes a neat edge all by itself. You'll only need to weave in the ends at the beginning and end of the two-colour striped knitting.

You'll soon see a very tidy, fine stripe appear in your knitting.

You can see how this technique has been used to great effect on the Ladies' raglan jumper (see p.52), Girls' pinafore dress (see p.66), Versatile kiddies' jumper (see p.72) and Lengthways-striped scarf (see p.121).

How to count rows

If you are counting stitches on stocking stitch, look for the V-shapes. Each 'V' is one row if you count up the column.

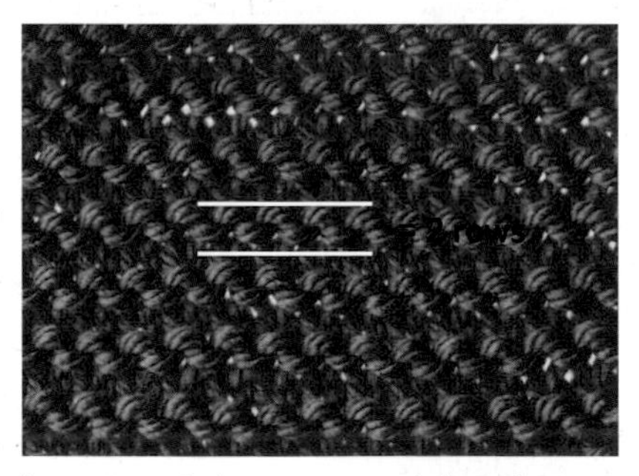

In garter stitch, you can see that there are ridges, each with a top and bottom part. Each ridge is two rows.

Markers

Sometimes a knitting pattern will ask you to place a marker – this is to help you with your pattern in upcoming rows.

Handy **HINT**

You don't need to go out and buy fancy markers. Simply take a piece of yarn in a contrasting colour to the yarn you are using (any oddment of DK yarn will do) and make a slip knot in it. Cut the yarn tails so they are only a couple of centimetres long when the loop is big enough to slip onto the needle, and there you go – a low-tech marker that I find much easier to use than some of the fancy beaded markers available, and a way of saving a few pennies at the same time.

PM = Place marker.
PM/SM = Pass marker/slip marker.
When you get to the marker in the next row, pass it from the left-hand needle to the right-hand needle without knitting it.

Tips for following knitting patterns

Sometimes a knitting pattern can seem as though it's written in Martian, but here are a few tips to help you on your way:

- Make a photocopy of the pattern so that you can scribble all your notes on it as you go.
- Then decide which size you want to knit.
- Go through your pattern with a highlighter pen, marking the instructions for your size throughout. (Knitting patterns print the instruction for the smallest size, followed by brackets that contain the instructions for the other sizes.) That way you'll cut out all the information you don't need, so you don't end up following the wrong instructions.
- Remember to knit a tension square if you're knitting an adult garment.
- Tick off rows as you go. That way, when you pick up your knitting you'll always know exactly where you are.

PROJECT 1

Adult booties

This is a pattern that I've been asked to design again and again by knitters who loved the baby bootie pattern in my first book.

It's a slightly more sophisticated version, which is still very easy to knit, but with an added sole. Perfect for padding around the house on cold winter days… just add pyjamas and a hot-water bottle for a perfect outfit to knit in.

GAUGE

An exact gauge isn't necessary for this project. Approximately 9sts in stocking stitch, using 10mm needles should give a 10cm square.

SIZE

One size (this should fit all adults)

ABBREVIATIONS

K = Knit

P = Purl

St(s) = Stitch(es)

St st = Stocking stitch

K2tog = Knit two stitches together

K2tog tbl = Knit two stitches together through the back of the loops

P2tog = Purl two stitches together

P2tog tbl = Purl two stitches together through the back of the loops

PM = Place marker

SM = Slip marker (slip the marker from the left-hand needle to the right-hand needle without knitting it)

1 x 1 rib = K1, P1 rib to end

Rep = Repeat

RS = Right side

WS = Wrong side

YOU WILL NEED

SUPER-BULKY YARN
such as Rowan Big Wool, Sirdar Bigga or Debbie Bliss Como. If you were using Rowan Big Wool, as shown in the photos here, you would need approximately 1.4 balls (so buy 2 balls and you'd have a bit left over).

107M YARN

10MM KNITTING NEEDLES

DARNING NEEDLE

START KNITTING

FOOT

Cast on 46sts.

K 1 row.

P23, PM, P to end.

K to 2sts before the marker, K2tog tbl, SM, K2tog, K to end. Count 44sts.

P to 2sts before the marker, P2tog, SM, P2tog tbl, P to end. Count 42sts.

Rep the last two rows until 22sts remain, ending with a purl row.

Work 1 x 1 rib for 10cm (you can remove the marker on the first rib row) ending with a RS row.

Cast off on WS (so the knit side of the foot is facing you) in pattern, leaving a long tail of yarn about 70cm long for sewing up with.

Here's what the finished foot of your bootie will look like before you sew it up.

SOLE

Cast on 10sts.

Work 1 x 1 rib to end.

Rep the last row until the piece measures 2cm less than the length of the sole of your foot – you can adjust this to your foot size the main body of the slipper will stretch to fit the sole when you come to sewing it up.

Cast off in pattern, leaving a long tail of yarn about 100cm for sewing up.

The bootie's sole.

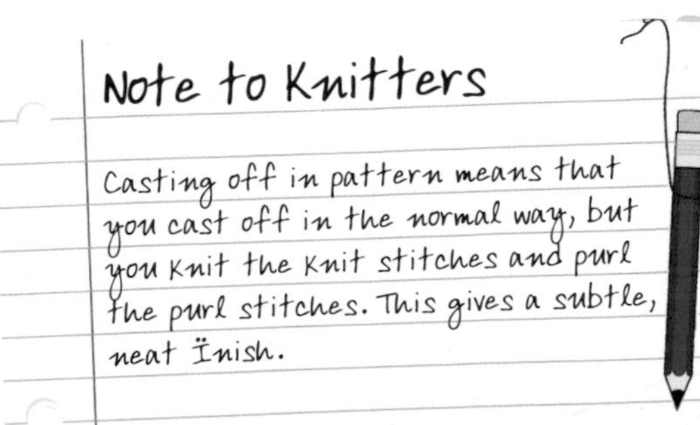

Note to Knitters

Casting off in pattern means that you cast off in the normal way, but you knit the knit stitches and purl the purl stitches. This gives a subtle, neat ïnish.

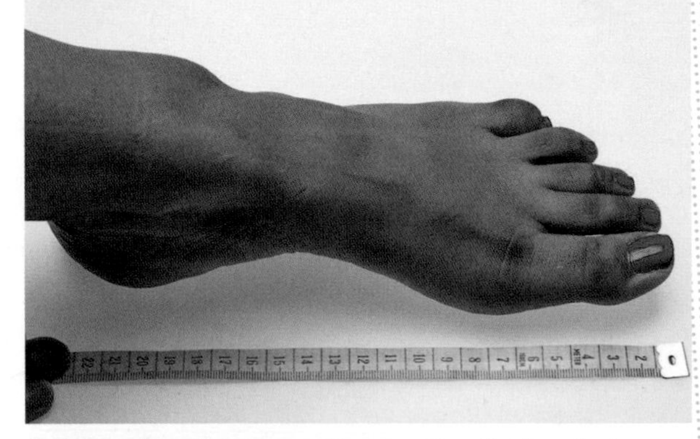

Knit the sole so it measures 2cm less than the length of your foot.

Making up

Fold the foot in half and sew up the back using mattress stitch. You can now see the slipper shape emerging.

To sew on the sole, turn the bootie inside out and use whip stitch to sew the sole to the foot.

The size of the sole will vary according to the length of your foot, but you can still make different sized soles fit into the foot by easing in as you sew (see p.37).

If you want a little more padding between your foot and the floor, simply slip an inner sole for a shoe into your bootie.

Ladies' raglan jumper

This is a pattern for a classic, simple ladies' jumper with a slightly fitted waist and fully fashioned raglan sleeves. A raglan sleeve is joined onto the body of a garment with a diagonal seam.

'Fully fashioned' means that the decreases are made a stitch or two in from the edge of the knitting, which gives a very tidy edge to your seams and makes the sewing-up process much more straightforward than it would be on non-fully fashioned seams.

Don't let the classic lines of this jumper fool you – you can jazz it up with colours, stripes, yarn choices and embellishments. It's the sort of garment you'll not only learn lots of neat knitting tricks on, but one that you'll wish you owned in lots of different colours, as its simple design looks good with everything! I hope that you will find this knitting project satisfying both to make and wear.

The fully fashioned raglan finish makes for a really neat seam. The size 12 jumper in this photo was knitted using 14 ½ balls of Debbie Bliss Alpaca Silk Aran. It's soooo soft and cosy!

YOU WILL NEED

ARAN-WEIGHT YARN
such as Debbie Bliss Alpaca Silk Aran or Sublime Cashmere Merino Silk Aran
Size 8–10: 729m
Size 12: 940m
Size 14–16: 1,162m
Size 18–20: 1,328m

5MM KNITTING NEEDLES

4.5MM KNITTING NEEDLES

4.5MM CIRCULAR NEEDLE, 40CM LONG

CROCHET HOOK
(I always suggest you use a hook one size smaller than the knitting needles)

DARNING NEEDLE

STITCH HOLDER

GAUGE

18sts and 24 rows in stocking stitch, using 5mm needles = 10cm square.

SIZE

8–10 (12, 14–16, 18–20)

ABBREVIATIONS

K = Knit

P = Purl

St(s) = Stitch(es)

St st = Stocking stitch

K2tog = Knit two stitches together

M1 = Make one stitch by picking up the loop in between two stitches

SSK = Slip, slip, knit

Cont = Continue

Rep = Repeat

Rem = Remaining

1 x 1 rib = K1, P1 rib to end

START KNITTING

BACK AND FRONT (the same)

Using 4.5mm needles, cast on 78 (90, 98, 106)sts.

Work 1 x 1 rib until work measures 4 (4, 5, 6)cm.

Change to 5mm needles and starting with a knit row, work st st until work measures 6 (8, 10, 10)cm from beginning, ending with a purl row.

Handy HINT

When changing needle sizes on the first knit row of the stocking stitch, the stitches will be on 4.5mm needles. Work that first knit row on to a 5mm needle, then discard the 4.5mm needles and continue with the 5mm needles.

WAIST SHAPING

Decrease row: K1, SSK, K to last 3sts, K2tog, K1. Count 76 (88, 96, 104)sts.

St st for 7 rows (P 1 row, K 1 row, P 1 row, K 1 row, P 1 row, K 1 row, P 1 row).

Decrease row: K1, SSK, K to last 3sts, K2tog, K1. Count 74 (86, 94, 102)sts.

St st for 7 rows (P 1 row, K 1 row, P 1 row, K 1 row, P 1 row, K 1 row, P 1 row).

Decrease row: K1, SSK, K to last 3sts, K2tog, K1. Count 72 (84, 92, 100)sts.

St st for 7 rows (P 1 row, K 1 row, P 1 row, K 1 row, P 1 row, K 1 row, P 1 row).

Decrease row: K1, SSK, K to last 3sts, K2tog, K1. Count 70 (82, 90, 98)sts.

St st for 7 rows (P 1 row, K 1 row, P 1 row, K 1 row, P 1 row, K 1 row, P 1 row).

Increase row: K1, M1, K to last st, M1, K1. Count 72 (84, 92, 100)sts

St st for 7 rows (P 1 row, K 1 row, P 1 row, K 1 row, P 1 row, K 1 row, P 1 row).

Increase row: K1, M1, K to last st, M1, K1. Count 74 (86, 94, 102)sts.

St st for 7 rows (P 1 row, K 1 row, P 1 row, K 1 row, P 1 row, K 1 row, P 1 row).

Increase row: K1, M1, K to last st, M1, K1. Count 76 (88, 96. 104)sts.

St st for 7 rows (P 1 row, K 1 row, P 1 row, K 1 row, P 1 row, K 1 row, P 1 row).

Increase row: K1, M1, K to last st, M1, K1. Count 78 (90, 98, 106)sts.

Starting with a purl row, continue in st st until piece measures 39 (43, 47, 50)cm from beginning, ending with a purl row – this is the length of your jumper from the underarm.

Note to Knitters

If you wish to shorten or lengthen the jumper to suit your body length, this is where to do it – I suggest that you alter the pattern by no more than 5cm, or the jumper will be too out of shape for the pattern. Don't forget to make the same alteration on both the front and the back of the jumper!

RAGLAN SHAPING

Cast off 2 (5, 7, 7)sts, K to end.
Count 76 (85, 91, 99)sts.

Cast off 2 (5, 7, 7)sts, P to end.
Count 74 (80, 84, 92)sts.

Decrease row: K1, SSK, K to last 3sts, K2tog, K1.
Count 72 (78, 82, 90)sts.

P 1 row.

BACK ONLY

Rep the last 2 rows until 32 (34, 34, 36)sts remain, ending with a purl row.

Transfer these stitches to a holder and set aside for now.

FRONT ONLY

Rep the last 2 rows until 54 (56, 60, 60)sts remain, ending with a purl row.

NECK SHAPING

(Please note that you will now be shaping the front for the neck AND continuing with the raglan shaping.)

K1, SSK, K17 (18, 19, 19). Cast off 14 (14, 16, 16)sts, K to last 3sts, K2tog, K1.

(To cast off in the middle of a row: knit the initial 17 (18, 19, 19)sts, THEN K1, K1, cast off the first knitted stitch and count 1, K1, cast off and count 2, and so on ... keep counting until you have counted 14 (14, 16, 16) cast-off stitches. Remember to count accurately!)

You now have 19 (20, 21, 21)sts on each side.

Working on the right side of the neck only (leaving the left side on the needle):

P 1 row.

Decrease row: SSK, K to last 3sts, K2tog, K1.

Rep the last 2 rows until 5 (4, 7, 5)sts remain, ending with a decrease row.

P 1 row.

K to last 3sts, K2tog, K1.

Rep the last 2 rows until 3sts remain, ending with a purl row.

K3tog.

Fasten off.

LEFT FRONT:

With WS of work facing you, rejoin yarn.

P 1 row.

K1, SSK, K to last 2sts, K2tog.
Rep the last 2 rows until 5 (4, 7, 5)sts remain, ending with a decrease row.

P 1 row.

K1, SSK, K to end.

Rep the last 2 rows until 3sts remain, ending with a purl row.

K3tog.

Fasten off.

Note to Knitters

HOW TO REJOIN YARN

STEP 1: Using a crochet hook, pull a strand of yarn through the nearest space below the first stitch on the needle.

STEP 2: Tie that into a knot with itself.

STEP 3: Use the long tail of the yarn to continue knitting.

STEP 4: When you've finished the knitting, weave the short tail of the yarn into the back of the work.

SLEEVES (make two the same)

Using 4.5mm needles, cast on 38 (42, 46, 48)sts.

Work in 1 x 1 rib until the work measures 4cm.

Change to 5mm needles and starting with a knit row, begin st st.

Increase row: K1, M1, K to last st, M1, K1. Count 40 (44, 48, 50)sts.

St st for 7 rows (P 1 row, K 1 row, P 1 row, K 1 row, P 1 row, K 1 row, P 1 row).

Increase row: K1, M1, K to last st, M1, K1. Count 42 (46, 50, 52)sts.

Rep the last 8 rows until you have 54 (54, 54, 54) sts, ENDING WITH AN INCREASE ROW.

St st for 5 rows (P 1 row, K 1 row, P 1 row, K I row, P 1 row).

Increase row: K1, M1, K to last st, M1, K1. Count 56 (56, 56, 56)sts.

Rep the last 6 rows until you have 56 (66, 74, 80) sts, ending with an increase row (please note that you'll already have the correct number of stitches for the smallest size).

Continue in st st until sleeve measures 46 (50, 52, 52)cm, ending with a purl row.

RAGLAN SHAPING

Cast off 2 (5, 7, 7)sts, K to end. Count 54 (61, 67, 73)sts.

Cast off 2 (5, 7, 7)sts, P to end. Count 52 (56, 60, 66)sts.

Decrease row: K1, SSK, K to last 3sts, K2tog, K1. Count 50 (54, 58, 64)sts.

P 1 row.

Rep the last 2 rows until you have 10 (10, 10, 10) sts, ending with a knit row.

Cast off.

Making up

Sew the back raglan to the back of the sleeves using mattress stitch. Start from the underarm section, picking up the two 'V's of the stocking stitch, and work your way towards the neck. You'll pick up the centre bar along the diagonal edges.

Note to Knitters

Make sure you follow the line of the decrease – by this I mean that if you look closely, you can see a neat row of 'V's running up the edge you are sewing. Keep one full line of 'V's to the inside of your sewing line – this way, the lines on both sides of the seam will join together to make a Ïawless Ïnished seam.

Handy HINT

I always suggest that you sew the sleeves to the back first, then the front. This way, you can get used to the technique on the back and you'll be an expert on it by the time you get to the front of the jumper!

Then sew the front raglans to the fronts of the sleeves.

Pick up and knit for the neckband

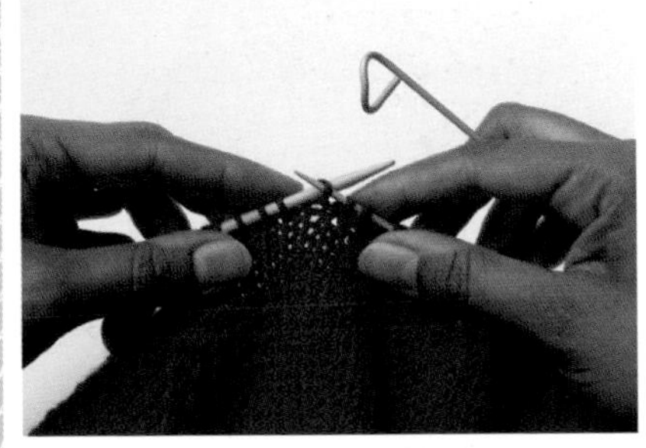

With the RS facing, transfer the centre back stitches to a straight 4.5mm needle. The point of the knitting needle will be facing the right-hand side of the back of the neck.

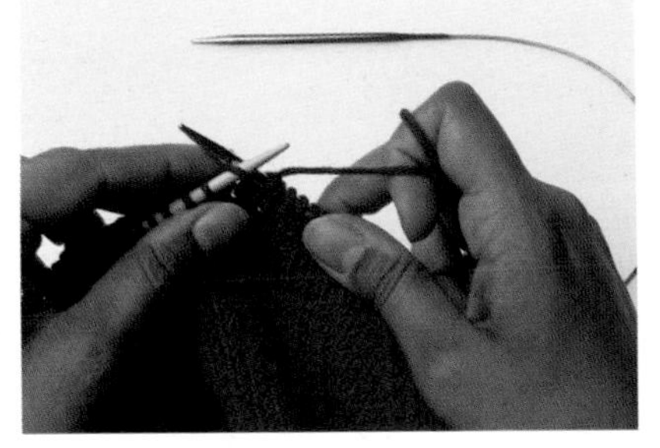

Work these stitches in 1 x 1 rib onto the circular needle.

Using the crochet hook, pick up and knit 8sts from the top of the left sleeve.

Pick up and knit 20 (21, 23, 23)sts down the left front.

Then 14 (14, 16, 18)sts across the cast-off stitches of the centre front.

Then 20 (21, 23, 23)sts up the right front.

Finally, pick up and knit 8sts across the top of the right sleeve.

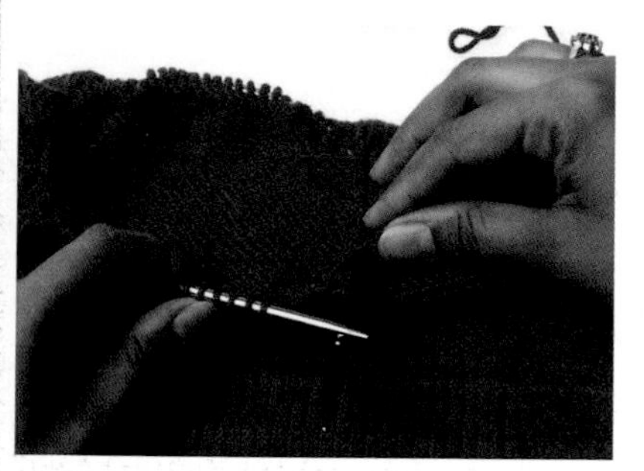

Count 104 (108, 114, 116)sts in total.

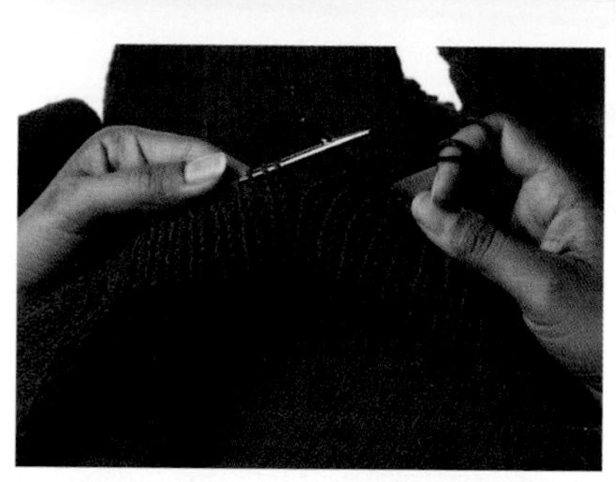

Join and work 1 x 1 rib until the neckband measures 4 (4, 5, 6)cm, ending the last round at the centre of the back of the neck.

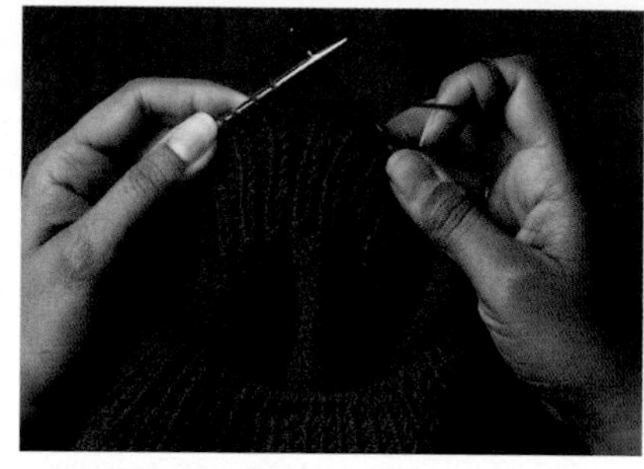

Turn – so that the WS of the work is facing you, and cast off in pattern.

(To cast off in pattern: K1, P1, cast off, K1, cast off, P1, cast off ... and so on, remembering to move the yarn back and forward depending on whether you are knitting or purling the next stitch. Fiddly, but worth it for extra neatness.)

You'll be left with a small gap where you end the cast-off of the neckband. Simply thread the tail of yarn onto a darning needle and sew up the gap with a couple of stitches before weaving the end into the inside of your knitting.

Side and underarm seams

Using mattress stitch, sew up the side and underarm seams. Always start from the underarm and sew towards the wrist, then go back to the underarm and sew down towards the waist. You'll be using a simple centre bar mattress stitch. This is the easiest way to get a tidy seam.

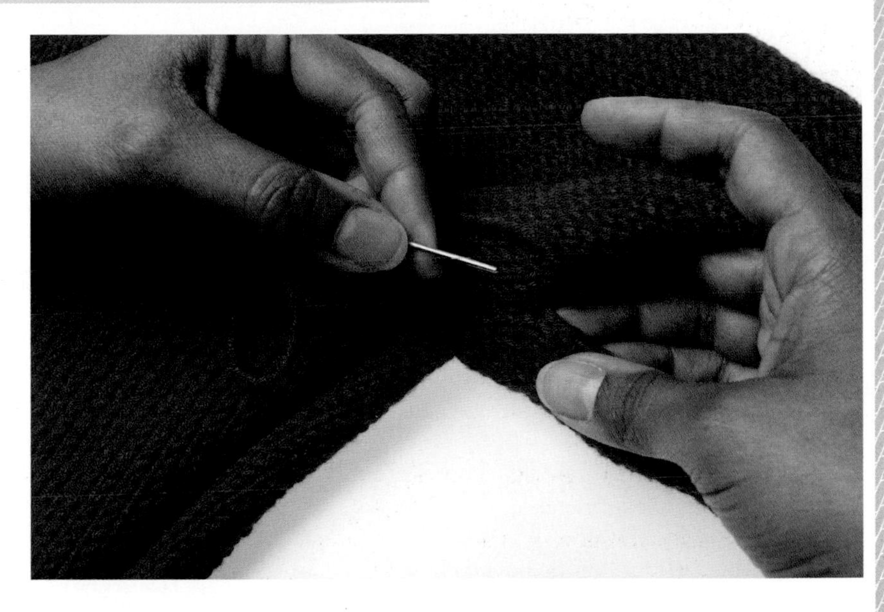

Now for the dull bit ... sit yourself in front of a good film and spend a rainy afternoon weaving in all those pesky ends! A tidy finish is worth its weight in gold and can really add that professional edge to your knitting.

Want an instant change of neckline? Cast on 100sts using 4.5mm needles and work in stocking stitch for around 15–20cm. Cast off. Sew your knitting into a tube and you have a slip-on polo-neck! You can also knit this in the round (see p.100).

This knitter personalised her jumper by knitting the body and sleeves using two-row colour changes with solid-colour ribbed borders (see p.45).

PROJECT 3

Men's bulky jumper

This jumper will knit up in no time using super-bulky yarn.

If you are just learning about shaping and sewing up, I think you'll like seeing it grow quickly, and the big yarn and needles will make the sewing-up process much easier as you'll really be able to see into the nooks and crannies of the fabric.

This is a great project for building up your confidence with knitting adult garments.

This jumper isn't just for the boys; I can see it being cosy winter wear for girls, too!

YOU WILL NEED

SUPER-BULKY YARN such as Rowan Big Wool, Sirdar Bigga or Debbie Bliss Como
36 inch chest: 571m
38 inch chest: 583m
40 inch chest: 611m

10MM KNITTING NEEDLES

12MM KNITTING NEEDLES

CROCHET HOOK
(I always suggest using a hook one size smaller than the knitting needles)

DARNING NEEDLE

Sewing up is easier on big knitting as you can really see the stitches. The size 38 jumper in the photo was knitted using just under 8 balls of Rowan Big Wool.

GAUGE

9sts in stocking stitch, using 10mm needles = 10cm square.

SIZE

Chest size (inches) 36 (38, 40)

ABBREVIATIONS

K = Knit
P = Purl
St(s) = Stitch(es)
St st = Stocking stitch
2 x 2 rib = K2, P2 rib to end
K2tog = Knit two stitches together
M1 = Make one stitch by picking up the loop in between two stitches
SSK = Slip, slip, knit
Cont = Continue
Rep = Repeat
Rem = Remaining

START KNITTING

BACK AND FRONT (the same until *)**

Using 10mm needles, cast on 44 (44, 48)sts.

Work 2 x 2 rib until work measures 7 (7, 8)cm.

Change to 12mm needles.

Size 38 only: K1, M1, K to last st, M1, K1.

All other sizes: K 1 row.

Count 44 (46, 48)sts.

Starting with a purl row, work st st until piece measures 41 (42, 43)cm from beginning, ending with a purl row.

***

BACK ONLY

SHAPE ARMHOLES

Cast off 3sts, K to end. Count 41 (43, 45)sts.

Cast off 3sts, P to end. Count 38 (40, 42)sts.

K2, SSK, K to last 4sts, K2tog, K2. Count 36 (38, 40)sts.

P 1 row.

K2, SSK, K to last 4sts, K2tog, K2. Count 34 (36, 38)sts.

Rep the last 2 rows until you have 6 (8, 8)sts, ending with a knit row.

Cast off on the WS of your work.

FRONT ONLY

SHAPE ARMHOLES

Cast off 3sts, K to end. Count 41 (43, 45)sts.

Cast off 3sts, P to end. Count 38 (40, 42)sts.

K2, SSK, K to last 4sts, K2tog, K2. Count 36 (38, 40)sts.

P 1 row.

Rep the last 2 rows until you have 24 (26, 26) sts, ending with a purl row.

SHAPE NECK OPENING

K2, SSK, K6 (6, 6), cast off 4 (6, 6) sts, K to last 4sts, K2tog, K2.

(To cast off in the middle of a row: knit the initial 6 (6, 6)sts, THEN K1, K1, cast off the first knitted stitch and count 1, K1, cast off and count 2, and so on ... keep counting until you have counted 4 (6, 6) cast-off stitches. Remember to count accurately!)

You will now work on each side of the neck separately.

Handy HINT

When changing needle sizes, on the first knit row of the stocking stitch, you'll have the stitches on 10mm needles. Work that first knit row on to 12mm needles, then discard the 10mm needles and continue with the 12mm needles.

RIGHT SIDE

P 1 row.

K2tog, K to last 4sts, K2tog, K2.

P 1 row.

K2tog, K to last 2sts, K2tog.

P 1 row.

K to last 2sts, K2tog.

Rep last 2 rows until 2sts remain.

K2tog, fasten off.

LEFT SIDE

With WS facing, rejoin yarn and P 1 row.

K2, SSK, K to last 2sts, K2tog.

P 1 row.

K2tog, K to last 2sts, K2tog.

P 1 row.

K2tog, K to end.

Rep last 2 rows until 2sts remain.

K2tog, fasten off.

I find it really helpful to tick off rows as I've knitted them, so I always know where I am when I pick up my knitting.

SLEEVES

Using 10mm needles, cast on 24 (24, 24)sts.

Work 2 x 2 rib for 7 (7, 8)cm.

Change to 12mm needles.

K1, M1, K to last st, M1, K1. Count 26 (26, 26)sts.

St st for 5 rows (P 1 row, K 1 row, P 1 row, K 1 row, P 1 row).

K1, M1, K to last st, M1, K1. Count 28 (28, 28)sts.

St st for 5 rows (P 1 row, K 1 row, P 1 row, K 1 row, P 1 row).

K1, M1, K to last st, M1, K1. Count 30 (30, 30)sts.

St st for 7 rows (P 1 row, K 1 row, P 1 row, K 1 row, P 1 row, K 1 row, P 1 row).

Rep last 8 rows until you have 36 (38, 38)sts.

Cont in st st until piece measures 47 (48, 49)cm from beginning, ending with a purl row.

ARMHOLE SHAPING

Cast off 3sts, K to end. Count 33 (35, 35)sts.

Cast off 3sts, P to end. Count 30 (32, 32)sts.

K2, SSK, K to last 4sts, K2tog, K2. Count 28 (30, 30)sts.

P 1 row.

K 1 row.

P 1 row.

K2, SSK, K to last 4sts, K2tog, K2. Count 26 (28, 28)sts.

P 1 row.

K 1 row.

P 1 row.

K2, SSK, K to last 4sts, K2tog, K2. Count 24 (26, 26) sts.

P 1 row.

RIGHT SLEEVE

Rep the last 2 rows until you have 10 (10, 10)sts, ending with a purl row.

Cast off 2sts, K to last 4sts, K2tog, K2. Count 7 (7, 7)sts.

P 1 row

K2tog, K to last 4sts, K2tog, K2. Count 5 (5, 5)sts.

P to last 2sts, P2tog. Count 4 (4, 4)sts.

K2tog, K to end. Count 3 (3, 3)sts.

Cast off.

LEFT SLEEVE

Rep the last 2 rows until you have 10 (10, 10)sts, ending with a knit row.

Cast off 2sts, P to end. Count 8 (8, 8)sts.

K2, SSK, K to end. Count 7 (7, 7)sts.

P2tog, P to end. Count 6 (6, 6)sts.

K2, SSK, K to end. Count 5 (5, 5)sts.

P2tog, P to end. Count 4 (4, 4)sts.

K2, SSK, K to end. Count 3 (3, 3)sts.

Cast off.

Making up

Note to Knitters

When sewing up this type of raglan seam (where the shaping is done two stitches in from the edge), look for two complete stitches ('V's) before picking up the centre bar towards the edge of the knitted piece.

Step 1: Using mattress stitch, sew the right back raglan to the back of the right sleeve.

Step 2: Sew the front of the right sleeve to the right front raglan.

Step 3: Sew the left front raglan to the front of the left sleeve.

Step 4: Sew the left back raglan to the back of the left sleeve.

Neckband

You will now pick up and knit the neckband. This is done in two parts: first the back, then the front.

Note to Knitters

The picked-up stitches around the neck will be close together at the back neckband and further apart from each other at the front. Just make sure that you space the stitches as equally as possible.

Back neckband

With RS facing, using 10mm needles and starting at the centre of the right sleeve, pick up 18 (18, 22)sts, working across the back of the jumper and ending at the centre of the left sleeve.

WS: P2, K2, rep to end.

RS: K2, P2, rep to end.

Rep last 2 rows until the neckband measures 7 (7, 8)cm, ending with a RS row. Cast off loosely on the WS in pattern. Leave a long tail of yarn for sewing up (about 30cm).

Front neckband

With RS facing, using 10mm needles and starting at the centre of the left sleeve, pick up 22 (22, 22)sts, working across the front of the jumper and ending at the centre of the right sleeve.

WS: P2, K2, rep to end.

RS: K2, P2, rep to end.

Repeat the last 2 rows until the neckband measures 7 (7, 8)cm, ending with a RS row. Cast off loosely on the WS in pattern. Leave a long tail of yarn for sewing up (about 30cm).

Sew up the side seams of the neck-band.

Sew up the underarm and side seams. Start sewing from the underarm and work towards the wrist, then go back and start from the underarm and sew up towards the waist.

This is the easiest way of ensuring that the underarms join up neatly.

Weave in all ends.

PROJECT 4

Girls' pinafore dress

Here's a pattern that I really enjoyed designing. It appeared nearly fully formed in my head, and I had instant visions of it being worn everywhere from the beach, to a winter party or a wedding.

This dress combines unfussy lines with a pretty frill; you can choose colour combinations to suit your little lady and accessorise the pattern with anything from knitted flowers to buttons and sequins.

The frill at the bottom produces a really tidy edge, and gives a weight to the skirt that makes it hang elegantly. The straps can be adjusted to suit, so that you can fit it to your girl as she grows taller (if it starts to look too short, you could extend its life by pairing it with trousers underneath, or with bright tights and wellies).

You can knit the dress in any double knit yarn – the most widely available of weights. I love it in cotton for summer, warm wool for winter, and what about a silk or bamboo yarn for a special occasion? Perfect!

You can knit the dress using a two-row colour stripe for a pretty effect. 5½ balls of the luxurious Debbie Bliss Amalfi makes this dress for a girl aged 4–5 years. I think it's elegant enough to be a bridesmaid's dress!

YOU WILL NEED

ANY STANDARD DOUBLE KNIT YARN, so you have lots of choice. I suggest a lovely, drapey cotton for summer dresses (I like Sublime Soya Cotton, Debbie Bliss Amalfi or Rowan Purelife), or a warm wool for a winter dress, worn with a long-sleeved T-shirt underneath (I suggest Rowan Handknit Wool or Debbie Bliss Cashmerino DK).
Age 1–2 years: 306m
Age 3–4 years: 477m
Age 4–5 years: 524m

4MM KNITTING NEEDLES

4MM CIRCULAR NEEDLE 80CM LONG, for the frill (optional)

CROCHET HOOK

DARNING NEEDLE

4 SMALL BUTTONS, approx. 1cm in diameter

NEEDLE AND THREAD

GAUGE

22sts and 30 rows in stocking stitch, using 4mm needles = 10 cm square.

SIZE

1–2 years (3–4 years, 4–5 years)

ABBREVIATIONS

K = Knit

P = Purl

St(s) = Stitch(es)

St st = Stocking stitch

K2tog = Knit two stitches together

KFB = Knit into the front and back of a stitch

SSK = Slip, slip, knit

YF = Yarn forward

Cont = Continue

Rep = Repeat

RS = Right side

WS = Wrong side

Have fun with your buttons! You'll need about 4½ balls of the lovely Soya Cotton DK by Sublime and ladybird buttons for a summer play-dress in size 3–4 years.

I've written the pattern to be knitted in two colours, like the example below: the first colour is indigo for the frill and bodice, and the second colour is turquoise for the skirt and straps, but you can use whichever colour combination appeals. If you like, you can make the dress in a single colour, or stripe in two or as many colours as you like. Use this pattern as a template to design your own dress!

START KNITTING

BACK AND FRONT (the same until *)**

FRILL

Using 4mm needles and the first colour, cast on 76 (94, 102)sts.

Starting with a knit row, work in st st for 7 rows, ending with a knit row.

WS: K 1 row – this is your first fold line.

RS: KFB, rep to end. Count 152 (188, 204)sts.

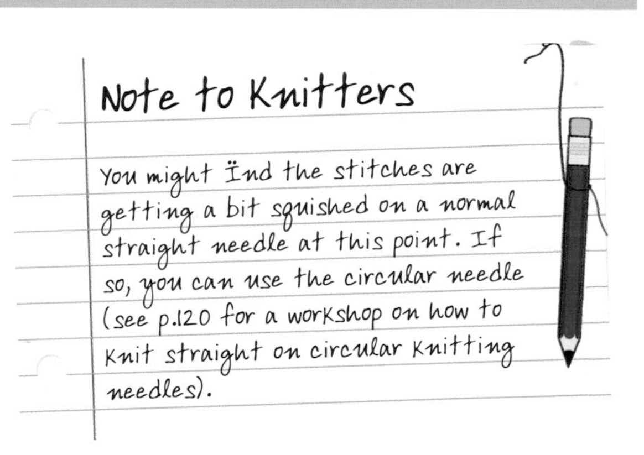

Starting with a purl row, work in st st for 7 rows, ending with a purl row.

RS: K2tog, rep to end. Count 76 (94, 102) sts.

WS: K 1 row – this is the sewing guideline.

SKIRT

Changing to your second colour of yarn, and starting with a knit row, work in st st for 4 rows, ending with a purl row.

Decrease row: K1, SSK, knit to last 3sts, K2tog, K1. Count 74 (92, 100)sts.

Starting and ending with a purl row, work in st st for 3 rows.

Decrease row: K1, SSK, knit to last 3sts, K2tog, K1. Count 72 (90, 98)sts.

Rep last 4 rows until 50 (58, 62)sts remain.

Cont in st st until piece measures 26 (34, 38)cm from first fold line, ending with a purl row.

Change back to first colour and K 1 row, then P 1 row.

BODICE

RS: K2, P2, rep to last 2sts - start and finish this row with K2.

WS: P2, K2, rep to last 2sts - start and finish this row with P2.

***

BACK ONLY

Rep the last 2 rows until you have 4 (6, 7)cm of rib, ending with a RS row.

Cast off in pattern on the WS of the work. Casting off in pattern means that you cast off in the normal way, but you knit the knit stitches and purl the purl stitches. This gives a subtle, neater finish.

FRONT ONLY

Rep the last 2 rows until you have 4 (6, 7)cm, ending with a WS row.

UNDERARM CAST-OFF

Cast off 4sts in pattern, rib to end. Count 46 (54, 58)sts.

Cast off 4sts in pattern, rib to end. Count 42 (50, 54)sts.

RS: K2, P2, rep to last 2sts - start and finish this row with K2.

WS: P2, K2, rep to last 2sts - start and finish this row with P2.

Rep the last 2 rows until you have 12 (13, 14)cm of rib in total, ending with a RS row.

Cast off on the WS of the work in pattern.

STRAPS

Using 4mm needles and the second colour (same as the frill), cast on 12sts.

RS: K5, P2, K5.

WS: P5, K2, P5.

Buttonhole row: K2, YF, K2tog, K1, P1, K2, YF, K2tog, K2. Count 12sts.

WS: P5, K2, P5.

RS: K5, P2, K5.

Rep the last 2 rows until the strap is approximately 20 (23, 26)cm long, ending with a RS row. Cast off, leaving a long tail of yarn for sewing up (about 30cm).

This dress works for all seasons and occasions, depending on how you dress it up or down.

Making up

Using mattress stitch, sew up the side seams of the dress.

Note to Knitters

When you sew up the bodice, make sure the top of the back lines up with the underarm of the front.

Hem

To make the frill, you need to fold it under at the first fold line and sew up using whip stitch.

The frill will fold up easily where it's supposed to. Uncurl it, and sew it up using whip stitch by simply taking a loop from the line where the frill joins the skirt – the sewing guide line – and a loop from the cast-on edge of the frill. See p.36 for whip stitch.

Weave in all your ends neatly.

Sew on buttons so that they are extra-secure. I don't want to hear stories of little girls pulling off their buttons and stuffing them up their noses!

Sew strap

Sew the strap securely to the back bodice.

The weight of the frill adds a pretty detail to this simple pinafore dress. This size 1–2 years dress uses just under 3 balls of Debbie Bliss Cashmerino DK.

Handy HINT

It's a good idea to knit the strap a little longer than you need and sew the excess into the back of the dress. Then, as the girl grows taller, the straps can be unsewn and re-sewn to the dress at a longer length so you can get more wear out of it. My experience is that small children generally grow taller more quickly than they grow wider, and the width of the dress will fit for a longer time than the length.

Feel free to personalise the dress to suit your little lady:

- Knit flowers to sew on
- Sew sequins or coloured buttons scattered across the skirt
- Knit colour stripes
- Knit a matching headband or handbag for a complete outfit.

Handy HINT

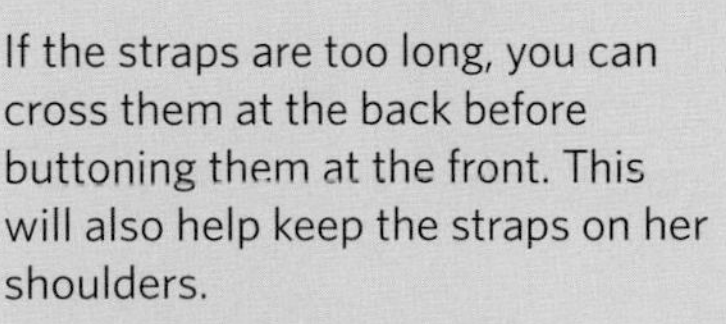

If the straps are too long, you can cross them at the back before buttoning them at the front. This will also help keep the straps on her shoulders.

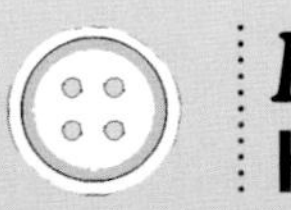

Handy HINT

If you find that the buttonhole is too big or loose for the button you've chosen, you can tighten it up by sewing some small stitches around it using sewing thread.

Versatile kiddies' jumper

OK ... are you paying attention? There's a lot of information coming your way in this versatile jumper-hoodie-or-not-which-different-shoulder style-are-you-knitting?

'Versatile' is the operative word here. Depending on which size of garment you knit, you will learn how to knit a drop shoulder, modified drop shoulder, hood, simple slashed neckline, long sleeves and short sleeves.

The sizes on offer fit children aged 0–3 months, 1–2 years, 3–4 years and 4–5 years. As with all children's clothing, if you aren't sure, opt for a bigger size – the child in question will definitely grow, and we don't want him or her to grow faster than your knitting!

Size	Neck	Shoulder
0-6 months	slash neck	drop shoulder
1-2 years	hood	drop shoulder
3-4 years	hood	modified drop shoulder
4-5 years	hood	modified drop shoulder

The smallest size, 0–3 months, is the simplest to make. Essentially, it consists of two rectangles for the body. The basic skills involved are ribbing, increasing and sewing up. This would make a great first foray into knitting garments if you'd like to knit something for a new baby that's not too taxing, where you can add personality with embroidery, colour, stripes, combinations, etc.

The next size up, 1–2 years, is slightly higher on the complication rating, as it has a hood. You'll need to learn how to pick up and knit, and you'll use a three-needle bind-off for the hood – one of my favourite techniques for a tidy finish.

The bigger sizes have a hood and a modified drop shoulder for a slightly more fitted look. This is essentially a big and baggy jumper, but the indented sleeve means that the fit around the shoulder has a more compact shape.

Drop shoulder.

Modified drop shoulder.

Questions & Answers

What's she talking about? Modified, drop a whatchamacallit?

A drop shoulder is the simplest sort of shape when knitting a jumper or cardigan. It basically means that the body and the top of the sleeve are simple rectangles with no shaping to make them fit together. You'll never get a sleek, fitted look with this technique, but I love it for making comfortable kids' clothing as it gives them room to move and grow.

A modified drop shoulder is a slightly more fitted version, in that the sleeve is set into the body by means of a simple 'notch' cast off into the body where the sleeve is sewn in.

Personalise your hoodie with different sleeve options or even a bit of freestyle embroidery on the front.

The self-patterning yarn Artesano Hummingbird DK gives a unique look to this jumper. The size 1–2 years size only requires 1½ skeins of this extra-long yarn.

YOU WILL NEED

LOOK FOR DOUBLE KNIT YARN, which comes in limitless options of colours and fibres. My test knitters enjoyed the smooth comfort of Debbie Bliss Cashmerino DK, the funky, self-patterning colours of Artesano Hummingbird DK, stripes in Sirdar Click, and Debbie Bliss Amalfi for a cotton jumper for a summer baby.
0–6 months: 315m
1–2 years: 583m
3–4 years: 611m
4–5 years: 700m

4MM KNITTING NEEDLES

4MM CIRCULAR NEEDLES, any length (you won't be knitting in the round in this pattern)

DARNING NEEDLE

CROCHET HOOK: try using a 3mm or 3.5mm hook, as it will make the picking up a bit easier

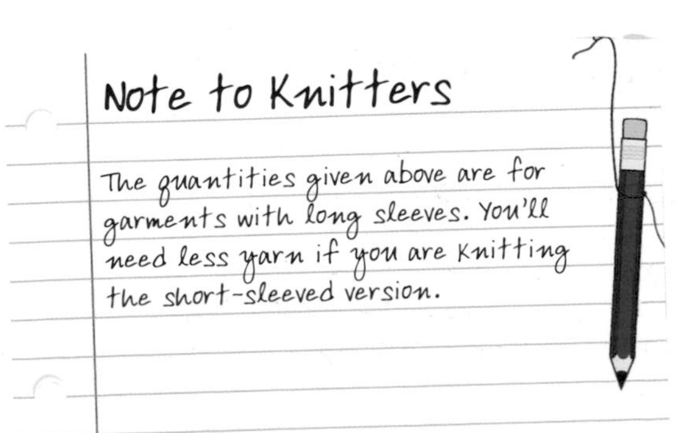

GAUGE

22sts and 30 rows in stocking stitch, using 4mm needles = 10cm square.

SIZES

0-6 months (1-2 years, 3-4 years, 4-5 years).

Please note that these garments are unisex and there will be a difference in size between, for example, a girl aged three and a boy of the same age. The best rule, when knitting for children, is that if you aren't sure, work bigger.

ABBREVIATIONS

K = Knit

P = Purl

St(s) = Stitch(es)

St st = Stocking stitch

1 x 1 rib = K1, P1 rib to end

K2tog = Knit two stitches together

M1 = Make one stitch by picking up the loop in between two stitches

Cont = Continue

Rep = Repeat

RS = Right side

WS = Wrong side

START KNITTING

BACK AND FRONT (the same to ***)

Cast on 58 (68, 74, 86)sts.

Work in 1 x 1 rib until piece measures 3 (4, 4, 5)cm.

***

BACK ONLY

Starting with a knit row, work in st st until piece measures 30 (32, 26, 29)cm from beginning, ending with a knit row.

Note to Knitters

The measurements for the body piece might seem a bit odd, with the bigger sizes having less length than the smaller sizes, but that's because they have decreases at the underarm for the modiﬁed drop shoulder.

Sizes 0-6 months and 1-2 years

Cast off.

Note to Knitters

The instructions for the ﬁrst two sizes: 0-6 months and 1-2 years, are included in knitting patterns as '-' because they have been cast off already and you don't have to take any action.

Sizes 3-4 and 4-5 years

UNDERARM FOR MODIFIED DROP SHOULDER

Cast off - (-, 6, 8)sts, P to end. Count - (-, 68, 78) sts.

Cast off - (-, 6, 8)sts, K to end. Count - (-, 62, 70) sts.

Starting with a purl row, cont in st st until piece measures - (-, 39, 43)cm from beginning, ending with a knit row.

Cast off on the WS.

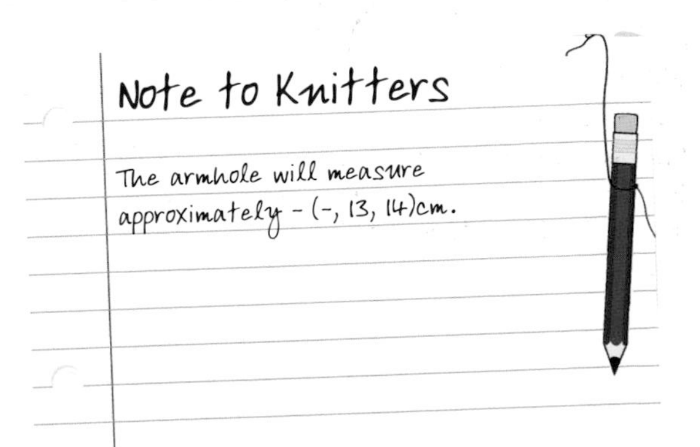

FRONT ONLY

Jumper for age 0–6 months only: the front and back are the same. This size has a slash neck opening and no hood.

All other sizes

Starting with a knit row, work in st st until piece measures – (26, 26, 29)cm from beginning, ending with a purl row.

Sizes 3–4, 4–5

UNDERARM FOR MODIFIED DROP SHOULDER

Cast off – (–, 6, 8)sts, K to end. Count – (–, 68, 78) sts.

Cast off – (–, 6, 8)sts, P to end. Count – (–, 62, 70) sts.

All sizes except 0–6 months

Starting with a knit row, cont in st st until piece measures – (26, 31, 36)cm from beginning, ending with a purl row.

SHAPE NECK OPENING

Separate for neck opening.

K – (26, 24, 26)sts, cast off – (16, 14, 18)sts, K to end. You will now have – (26, 24, 26)sts on either side of the neck.

(To cast off in the middle of a row: knit the initial – (26, 24, 26)sts, THEN K1, K1, cast off the first knitted stitch and count 1, K1, cast off and count 2, and so on … keep counting until you have counted – (16, 14, 18) cast-off stitches. Remember to count accurately!)

Now work the stitches on the right front of the neck, ignoring the left front for now – leave the stitches for the left front on the needle but don't knit them.

RIGHT FRONT

P – (26, 24, 26)sts (on the right front), turn.

K2tog, K to end. Count – (25, 23, 25)sts.

P 1 row.

Rep last 2 rows until – (21, 21, 21)sts remain on the right front.

Cont in st st until piece measures – (32, 39, 43)cm from beginning, ending with a knit row.

Cast off.

LEFT FRONT

Rejoin sts with WS of work facing you and P 1 row.

K to last 2sts, K2tog.

P 1 row.

Rep last 2 rows until – (21, 21, 21)sts remain on the left front.

Cont in st st until piece measures – (32, 39, 43)cm from beginning, ending with a knit row.

Cast off.

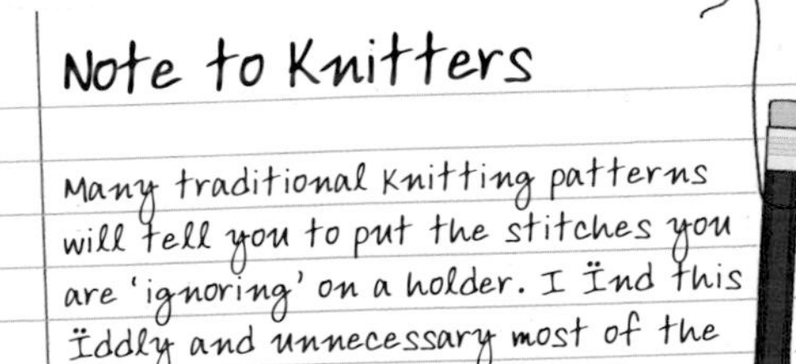

Making up

Using mattress stitch (and picking up the two sides of the 'V' - see p.32), sew up the shoulder seams. Start at the arm edge and sew your way in towards the neck edge.

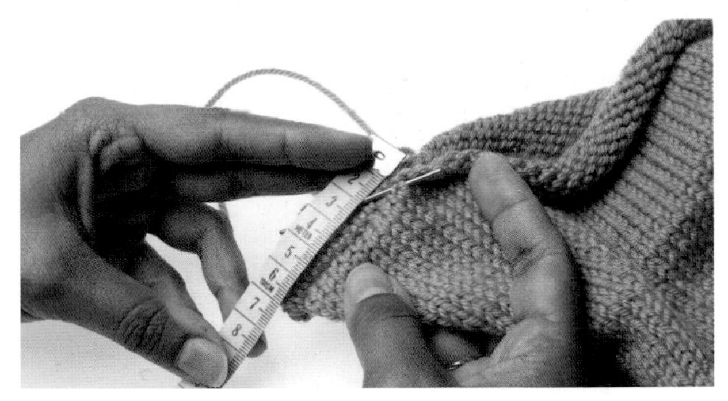

On the slash neck jumper, sew the shoulder seams for approximately 6cm from the armhole edge towards the neck opening.

Hood

With right side facing, using the 4mm circular needles, and starting at the right-hand (as it's worn) edge of the cast-off stitches on the front of the neck opening, pick up and knit - (15, 19, 20)sts up the right front of the jumper, - (22, 24, 28)sts across the back of the neck, and - (15, 19, 20)sts down the left front (to the edge of the cast-off stitches). Please note that you will not be picking up stitches at the front cast-off edge of the neck opening.

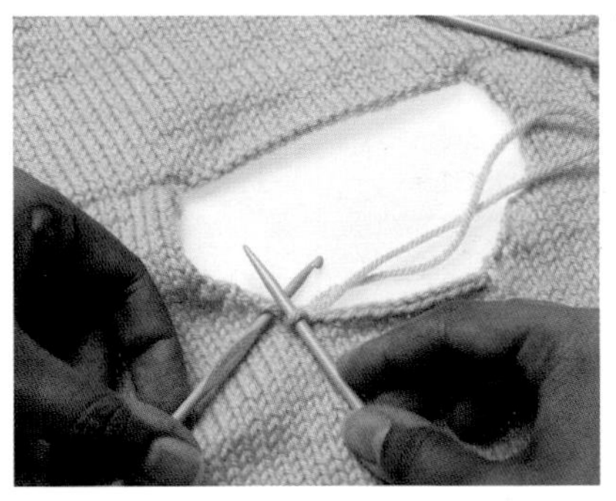

Start picking up and knitting at the slope of the right front.

Please note that you will not be picking up stitches at the front cast-off edge of the neck opening.

Count - (52, 62, 68)sts.
Work back and forth on the circular needle (without joining into a round - you use the needles as if they were normal straight needles - just ignore the fact that the stitches are all on one needle... trust me... it'll make sense when you do it!).
P 1 row.
Increase row: K - (16, 21, 22)sts, [M1, K2] - (10, 10, 12) times, K to end. Count - (62, 72, 80)sts.
Starting with a purl row, cont in st st until the hood measures - (23, 24, 25)cm from the neck, ending with a knit row.

Finish using the three-needle bind-off (see p.25).

Hood border

With right side facing, starting at the right neck front of the hood and using the 4mm circular needles, pick up and knit - (65, 67, 69)sts up the right front edge of the hood, and - (66, 68, 70)sts down the left front edge of the hood.

Count - (131, 135, 139)sts.

Row 1 (WS): P1, K1, repeat to end (start and end this row with a P1).

Row 2 (RS): K1, P1, repeat to end (start and end this row with a K1).

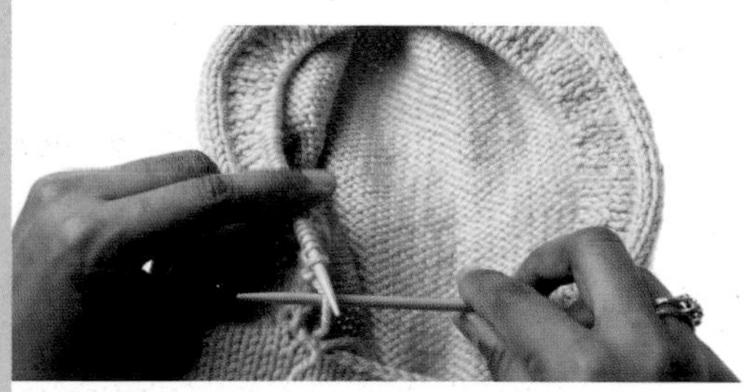

Repeat the last 2 rows a further - (2, 2, 3) times each; that is - (6, 6, 8) rows of rib in total, ending with a RS row.

Cast off in pattern on the wrong side of the work (remember to knit the knit stitches and purl the purl stitches as you cast off).

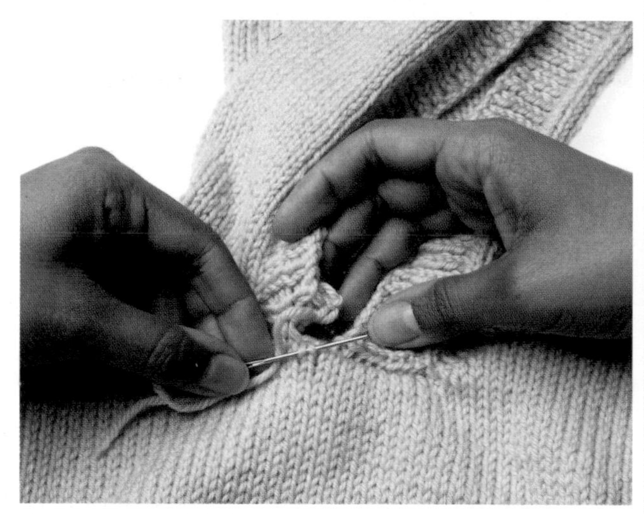

Sew the edges of the hood border to the open cast-off edge of the front of the neck opening. To be sure to get a neat finish, sew further away from the edge of the work rather than too near the cast-off edge on the front of the neck.

Sleeves

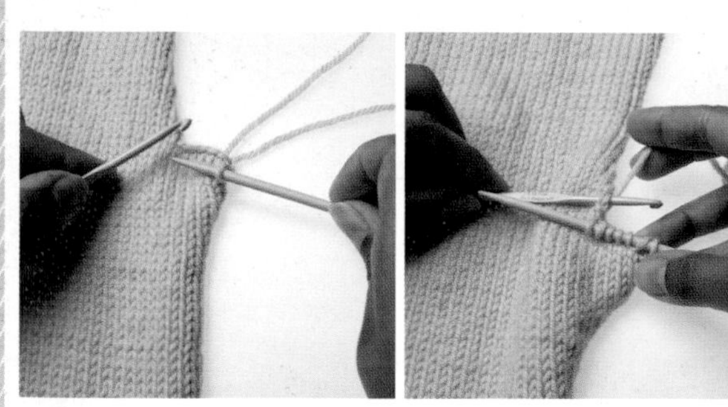

You'll notice you have to 'turn a corner' to pick up and knit for the short sleeves on the modified drop. Don't let this faze you!

SHORT SLEEVES (FOR A VEST TOP)

Sizes 0-6 months and 1-2 years have a drop shoulder rather than the modified drop shoulder of the other sizes, so are slightly different:

Pick up and knit 58 (66, -, -)sts for the short sleeve. Half of these will be on one side of the shoulder seam and half on the other.

Sizes 3-4, 4-5, years (for the modified drop shoulder):

Pick up and knit - (-, 6, 8)sts along the armhole cast-off, - (-, 35, 40)sts up the sleeve opening to the shoulder seam, - (-, 35, 40)sts down the sleeve opening on the other side of the shoulder seam and - (-, 6, 8)sts along the armhole cast-off.

Count 58 (66, 82, 96)sts in total.

Work in 1 x 1 rib for 2 (3, 3, 4)cm, ending with a RS row.

Cast off on WS in pattern.

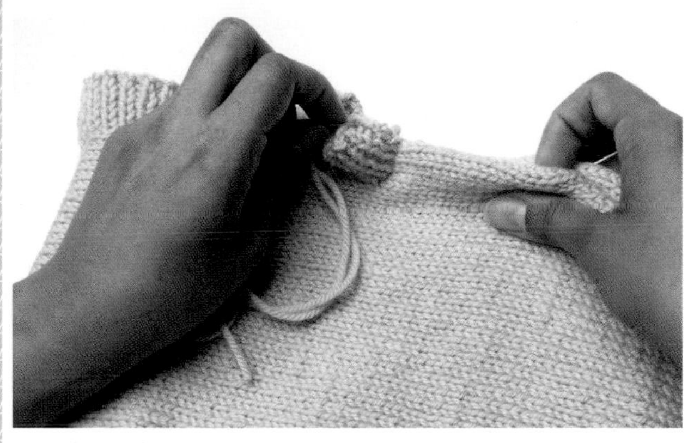
Sew the underarm and side seams using mattress stitch.

LONG SLEEVES (KNIT TWO THE SAME)

Cast on 30 (34, 40, 46)sts.
Work in 1 x 1 rib until piece measures 3 (4, 4, 5)cm.
K1, M1, K to last st, M1, K1. Count 32 (36, 42, 48)sts.
P 1 row.
K 1 row.
P 1 row.
K1, M1, K to last st, M1, K1. Count 34 (38, 44, 50)sts.
Rep last 4 rows until you have 58 (66, 70, 80)sts.
Cont in st st until sleeve measures 23 (24, 28, 30)cm from the beginning, ending with a knit row.
Cast off on the WS of the work.

Sew the sleeve into the armhole

Fold the sleeve in half and find the centre of the top of the sleeve.

Using a long piece of yarn (about 80cm) on a darning needle, pick up the two sides of the 'V' of the knitting on the centre of the sleeve.

Then, on the stitch nearest the shoulder seam on the body of the jumper, pick up the centre bar of the 'V'.

Sewing from the centre of the body and sleeve, working your way towards the underarm, sew the body and sleeve together using mattress stitch. You will pick up the centre bar on the body and the two lines of the 'V' on the sleeve.

Continue until you reach the cast-off stitches at the underarm – this is if you are knitting the size with the modified drop sleeve. If you aren't knitting the modified drop pattern, continue sewing up until you reach the underarm.

For the modified drop sleeve only, continue sewing around the 'corner' of the underarm – you will swap to picking up the 'V's on the body and the centre bar on the sleeve.

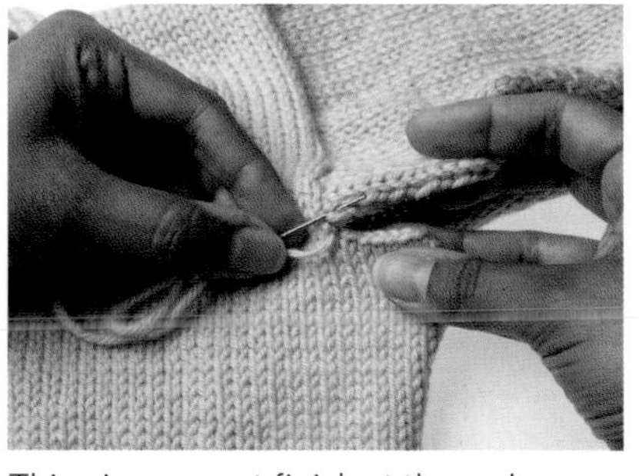
This gives a neat finish at the underarm.

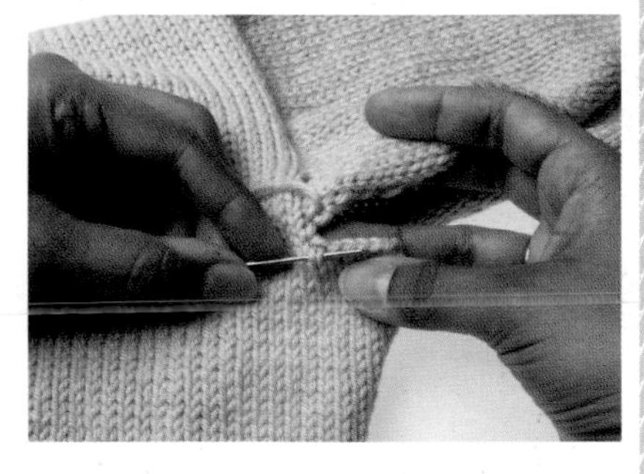

Then sew up the sleeve and body seams. Start from the underarm and sew the seam towards the cuff end of the sleeve. Then start sewing from the underarm and sew the seam towards the waist of the jumper. This ensures that the underarm seam has a tidy and accurate finish.

Weave in all the ends.

PROJECT 6

Ladies' classic cardigan

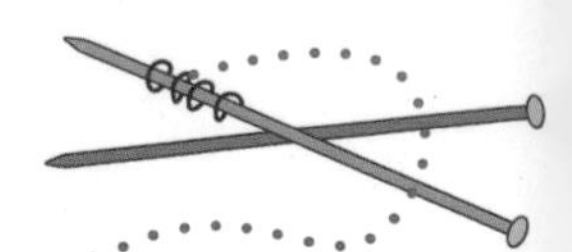

I'm a huge fan of The Cardigan. I own endless variations of this versatile layer and rarely leave the house without one.

I know that knitting in 4-ply yarn is a labour of love that some of you may run from, but I couldn't resist adding this pattern to the book for those of you who, like me, enjoy the commitment of a project that might take a bit longer to make, but ends up being just that little bit more satisfying. Students often ask me for a 'simple' cardigan pattern for beginners or intermediate knitters. I think that this pattern is the answer, and it comes with options to really make it something special and individual.

Personally, I plan to knit one of these in every colour and sleeve length combination that I can! I hope you'll take advantage of the options I've given to personalise this pattern.

Handy HINT

I suggest you always buy one more ball of yarn than you think you'll need when knitting a big project. Amounts needed can vary, and it's very disheartening to run out of yarn towards the end of a project and find it's no longer available.

Choose the sleeve length to suit you. In the photo, the pink cardigan is a size 8–10 with three-quarter-length sleeves and was knitted using just over 8 balls of Classic Yarns Siena. This is a mercerised cotton yarn, so it weighs a bit more than other yarns, but is still lovely and cool for summer. The long-sleeved cardigan is a size 18–20 and used 10 balls of Sublime Baby Cashmere Merino 4-ply Silk.

YOU WILL NEED

4-PLY YARN
You can choose the fibre to suit the season and experiment with colour; for example you could try a self-patterning sock yarn.

Size 8–10: short sleeves 975m, three-quarter sleeves 1,195m, long sleeves 1,590m
Size 12: short sleeves 1,075m, three-quarter sleeves 1,300m, long sleeves 1,725m
Size 14: short sleeves 1,190m, three-quarter sleeves 1,410m, long sleeves 1,850m
Size 16: short sleeves 1,400m, three-quarter sleeves 1,610m, long sleeves 2,050m
Size 18–20: short sleeves 1,645m, three-quarter sleeves 1,890m, long sleeves 2,330m

2.75MM KNITTING NEEDLES

3.25MM KNITTING NEEDLES

CROCHET HOOK – 3mm is a good size for this fine yarn

DARNING NEEDLE

11 (12, 12, 13, 14) BUTTONS approx. 1cm in diameter

MATCHING SEWING THREAD AND NEEDLE

Handy HINT

You can alter this cardigan pattern by varying the following:

- Sleeve length
- Self-striping yarn (such as sock yarn) will give an extra zing of colour
- Buttons ... one of the perks of knitting is the fun of choosing buttons!

GAUGE

28sts and 36 rows in stocking stitch, using 3.25cm needles = 10cm square.

SIZE

8–10 (12, 14, 16, 18–20)

ABBREVIATIONS

K = Knit

P = Purl

St(s) = Stitch(es)

St st = Stocking stitch

1 x 1 rib = K1, P1 rib to end

K2tog = Knit two stitches together

K2tog tbl = Knit two stitches together through the back of the loop

M1 = Make one stitch by picking up the loop in between two stitches

P2tog = Purl two stitches together

P2tog tbl = Purl two stitches together through the back of the loop

YF = Yarn forward

Rem = Remaining

Cont = Continue

RS = Right side

WS = Wrong side

START KNITTING

BACK

Using 2.75mm needles, cast on 120 (128, 136, 150, 156)sts.

Work in 1 x 1 rib for 10 rows.

Change to 3.25mm needles and starting with a knit row, work in st st until piece measures 35 (36, 37, 38, 39)cm from beginning, ending with a purl row.

Note to Knitters

This part of the cardigan may seem like a long, dull, samey expanse of stocking stitch ... well, it is! To combat the boredom, I suggest that you relax in front of a film and enjoy this part of the project as something you can knit with less concentration. I find that relaxing, rather than dull!

ARMHOLES

Cast off 4 (5, 5, 6, 6)sts, K to end. Count 116 (123, 131, 144, 150)sts.

Cast off 4 (5, 5, 6, 6)sts, P to end. Count 112 (118, 126, 138, 144)sts.

Decrease row 1 (RS): K2tog tbl, K to last 2sts, K2tog. Count 110 (116, 124, 136, 142)sts.

Decrease row 2 (WS): P2tog, P to last 2sts, P2tog tbl. Count 108 (114, 122, 134, 140)sts.
Rep the last 2 rows until 104 (110, 118, 126, 132)sts remain, ending with a WS row.

Decrease row 1 (RS): K2tog tbl, K to last 2sts, K2tog. Count 102 (108, 116, 124, 130)sts.

Purl 1 row.

Rep the last 2 rows until 92 (96, 100, 108, 112)sts remain.

Cont in st st until armhole measures 19 (20, 21, 23, 24)cm, ending with a knit row.

Cast off on the WS of your work.

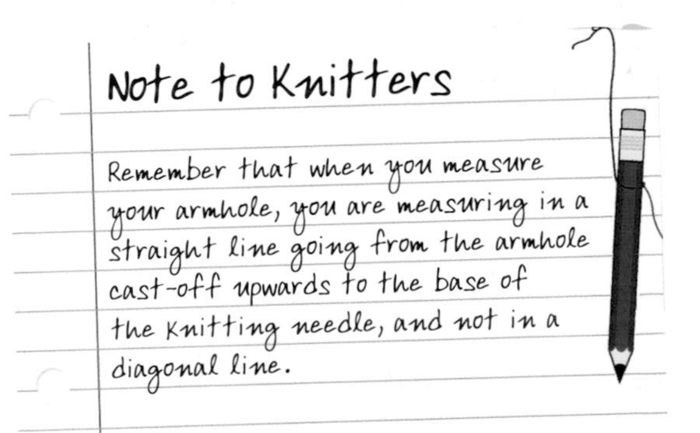

Handy HINT

Whilst working on this project, I suggest that you knit a few small or easy projects at the same time. That will stop you getting bored or bogged down with your big project, ensure you don't get pains in your hands from working with fine yarn for long periods, and give you the added satisfaction of finishing small projects in the meantime.

LEFT FRONT

Using 2.75mm needles, cast on 56 (60, 64, 72, 74) sts.

Work 1 x 1 rib for 10 rows.

Change to 3.25mm needles and starting with a knit row, work in st st until piece measures 35 (36, 37, 38, 39)cm from beginning, ending with a purl row.

ARMHOLE

Cast off 4 (5, 5, 7, 6)sts, K to end. Count 52 (55, 59, 65, 68)sts.

Purl 1 row.

Decrease row 1 (RS): K2tog tbl, K to end. Count 51 (54, 58, 64, 67)sts.

Decrease row 2 (WS): P to last 2sts, P2tog tbl. Count 50 (53, 57, 63, 66)sts.

Rep the last 2 rows until 48 (51, 55, 59, 62)sts remain, ending with a purl (WS) row.

K2tog tbl, K to end. Count 47 (50, 54, 58, 61)sts.

Purl 1 row.

Rep the last 2 rows until 42 (44, 46, 50, 52)sts remain, ending with a purl (WS) row.

Starting with a knit row, work in st st for 5 (7, 7, 11, 13) rows, ending with a knit (RS) row.

NECK

Cast off 7 (8, 9, 10, 11)sts, P to end. Count 35 (36, 37, 40, 41)sts.

Decrease row 1 (RS): K to last 2sts, K2tog. Count 34 (35, 36, 39, 40)sts.

Decrease row 2 (WS): P2tog, P to end. Count 33 (34, 35, 38, 39)sts.

Decrease row 1 (RS): K to last 2sts, K2tog. Count 32 (33, 34, 37, 38)sts.

Decrease row 2 (WS): P2tog, P to end. Count 31 (32, 33, 36, 37)sts.

Decrease row 1 (RS): K to last 2sts, K2tog. Count 30 (31, 32, 35, 36)sts.

P 1 row.

Rep the last 2 rows until 27 (28, 29, 32, 33) sts remain, ending with a purl row.

Decrease row 1 (RS): K to last 2sts, K2tog. Count 26 (27, 28, 31, 32) sts.

P 1 row.

K 1 row.

P 1 row.

Rep the last 4 rows until 22 (23, 24, 27, 28)sts remain.

Cont in st st until armhole measures 19 (20, 21, 23, 24)cm, ending with a knit row.

Cast off on WS of your work.

Handy HINT

Don't skimp on the length of your cardigan, as this will affect the button bands and buttonholes. Lay your work out flat to measure it, and if you aren't quite sure, work an extra couple of rows.

You can have fun and spend hours choosing your buttons! The short-sleeved cardigan in the photo is a size 16 and was knitted using just over 5 balls of the gorgeous Artesano Alpaca 4-ply.

RIGHT FRONT

Using 2.75mm needles, cast on 56 (60, 64, 72, 74) sts.

Work 1 x 1 rib for 10 rows.

Change to 3.25mm needles and starting with a knit row, work in st st until piece measures 35 (36, 37, 38, 39)cm from beginning, ending with a knit row.

ARMHOLE

Cast off 4 (5, 5, 7, 6)sts, P to end. Count 52 (55, 59, 65, 68)sts.

Decrease row 1 (RS): K to last 2sts, K2tog. Count 51 (54, 58, 64, 67)sts.

Decrease row 2 (WS): P2tog, P to end. Count 50 (53, 57, 63, 66)sts.

Rep the last 2 rows until 48 (51, 55, 59, 62)sts remain, ending with a purl (WS) row.

K to last 2sts, K2tog. Count 47 (50, 54, 58, 61)sts.

Purl 1 row.

Rep the last 2 rows until 42 (44, 46, 50, 52)sts remain, ending with a purl (WS) row.

Starting with a knit row, st st for 4 (6, 6, 10, 12) rows, ending with a purl (WS) row.

NECK

Cast off 7 (8, 9, 10, 11)sts, K to end. Count 35 (36, 37, 40, 41)sts.

P 1 row.

Decrease row 1 (RS): K2tog tbl, K to end. Count 34 (35, 36, 39, 40)sts.

Decrease row 2 (WS): P to last 2sts, P2tog, tbl. Count 33 (34, 35, 38, 39)sts.

Decrease row 1 (RS): K2tog tbl, K to end. Count 32 (33, 34, 37, 38)sts.

Decrease row 2 (WS): P to last 2sts, P2tog tbl. Count 31 (32, 33, 36, 37)sts.

Decrease row 1 (RS): K2tog tbl, K to end. Count 30 (31, 32, 35, 36)sts.

P 1 row.

Rep the last 2 rows until 27 (28, 29, 32, 33)sts remain, ending with a purl row.

Decrease row 1 (RS): K2tog tbl, K to end. Count 26 (27, 28, 31, 32)sts.

P 1 row.

K 1 row.

P 1 row.

Rep the last 4 rows until 22 (23, 24, 27, 28)sts remain.

Cont in st st until armhole measures 19 (20, 21, 23, 24)cm, ending with a knit row.

Cast off on WS of your work.

SLEEVES

The sleeves for the right and left arms are the same, but the start of the pattern varies, depending on the sleeve length that you choose.

SHORT SLEEVE (MAKE TWO THE SAME)

Using 2.75mm needles, cast on 72 (76, 80, 84, 88) sts.

Work 1 x 1 rib for 10 rows.

Changing to 3.25mm needles:

K 1 row.

P 1 row.

K1, M1, K to last st, M1, K1. Count 74 (78, 82, 86, 90)sts.

P 1 row.

K 1 row.

P1, M1, K to last st, M1, P1. Count 76 (80, 84, 88, 92)sts.

Rep the last 6 rows, stopping when you have 84 (90, 96, 106, 112)sts and ending on a P (K, P, K, P) row.

Work in st st for a further 6 (5, 6, 5, 4) rows, ending with a purl row.

Now move on to the armhole shaping instructions, which are the same for all sleeve lengths.

Note to Knitters

On a purl row, M1 is the same method as an increase on a knit row (see p.23).

THREE-QUARTER SLEEVE (MAKE TWO THE SAME)

Using 2.75mm needles, cast on 56 (58, 62, 68, 72) sts.

Work 1 x 1 rib for 10 rows.

Changing to 3.25mm needles:

K1, M1, K to last st, M1, K1. Count 58 (60, 64, 70, 74)sts.

P 1 row.

K 1 row.

P 1 row.

K1, M1, K to last st, M1, K1. Count 60 (62, 66, 72, 76)sts.

Rep the last 4 rows until you have 84 (90, 96, 106, 112)sts.

Cont in st st until sleeve measures 26 (27, 27, 28, 29)cm from the beginning, ending with a purl row.

Now move on to the armhole shaping instructions, which are the same for all sleeve lengths.

LONG SLEEVE (MAKE TWO THE SAME)

Using 2.75mm needles, cast on 68 (68, 72, 76, 76) sts.

Work 1 x 1 rib for 10 rows.

Changing to 3.25mm needles:

K1, M1, K to last st, M1, K1. Count 70 (70, 74, 78, 78)sts.

P 1 row.

K 1 row.

P 1 row.

K 1 row.

P 1 row.

K1, M1, K to last st, M1, K1. Count 72 (72, 76, 80, 80)sts.

Rep the last 6 rows until you have 84 (90, 96, 106, 112)sts.

Cont in st st until sleeve measures 43 (46, 46, 47, 48)cm from the beginning, ending with a purl row
Now move on to the armhole shaping instructions, which are the same for all sleeve lengths.

ARMHOLE SHAPING (THIS IS THE SAME FOR ALL SLEEVE LENGTHS)

Cast off 4 (5, 5, 6, 6)sts, K to end. Count 80 (85, 91, 100, 106)sts.

Cast off 4 (5, 5, 6, 6)sts, P to end. Count 76 (80, 86, 94, 100)sts.

Decrease row 1 (RS): K2tog tbl, K to last 2sts, K2tog. Count 74 (78, 84, 92, 98)sts.

Decrease row 2 (WS): P2tog, P to last 2sts, P2tog tbl. Count 72 (76, 82, 90, 96)sts.

Rep the last 2 rows until 68 (72, 78, 82, 88)sts remain.

Decrease row 1 (RS): K2tog tbl, K to last 2sts, K2tog. Count 66 (70, 76, 80, 86)sts.

P 1 row.

Rep last 2 rows until 56 (58, 60, 64, 68)sts remain.

Decrease row 1 (RS): K2tog tbl, K to last 2sts, K2tog. Count 54 (56, 58, 62, 66)sts.

Decrease row 2 (WS): P2tog, P to last 2sts, P2tog tbl. Count 52 (54, 56, 60, 64)sts.

Rep the last 2 rows until 20 (22, 20, 24, 24)sts remain.

Cast off 3sts, K to end. Count 17 (19, 17, 21, 21)sts.

Cast off 3sts, P to end. Count 14 (16, 14, 18, 18)sts.

Cast off 3sts, K to end. Count 11 (13, 11, 15, 15)sts.

Cast off 3sts, P to end. Count 8 (10, 8, 12, 12)sts.

Cast off remaining stitches.

Making up

Using mattress stitch, join the shoulder seams of the back to the left and right fronts. Start sewing at the armhole edge and work towards the direction of the neck opening to ensure that pieces fit together correctly.

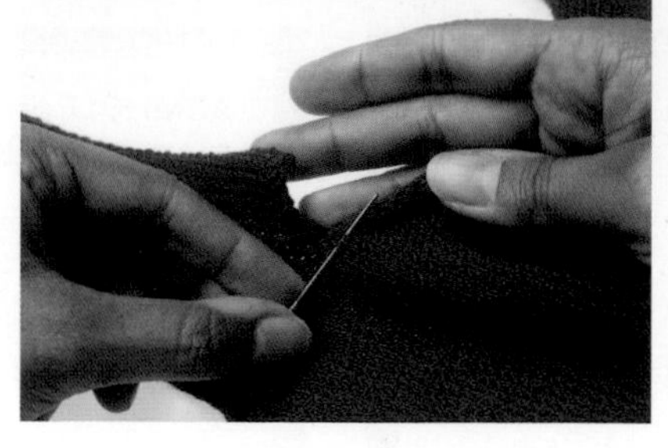

Handy HINT

This project will have taken you a while to knit, so be patient during the sewing up. Take your time and if you aren't happy with a particular seam, don't be afraid to pull it out and have another go. Remember to refer to the Sewing-up workshop on p.32 as you go.

Neckband

Using 2.75mm needles and with RS facing, pick up and knit:

50 (52, 54, 56, 58)sts up the right front of the neck,

49 (51, 53, 55, 57)sts along the back of the neck,

50 (52, 54, 56, 58)sts down the left front of the neck.

Count 149 (155, 161, 167, 173)sts.

Note to Knitters

If the neck and button bands seem to have too many stitches to squash onto a normal straight needle, you can knit them back and forth on 2.75mm circular needles. See p.120 for how to work straight on circular needles.

Row 1 (WS): P1, K1, rib to end (you'll start and end this row with a P1).

Row 2 (RS): K1, P1, rib to end (you'll start and end this row with a K1).

Rep the last 2 rows to a total of 10 rows, ending with a Row 2.

Cast off on WS of cardigan in pattern (remember to knit the knit stitches and purl the purl stitches when casting off in rib).

Handy HINT

When picking up stitches from a long length of knitting, I suggest that you mark out sections with dressmaking pins. Divide the section into eight equal parts and work out how many stitches you need to pick up in each section. This will ensure that you don't get to the end and discover you are way out on your numbers.

Left front button band

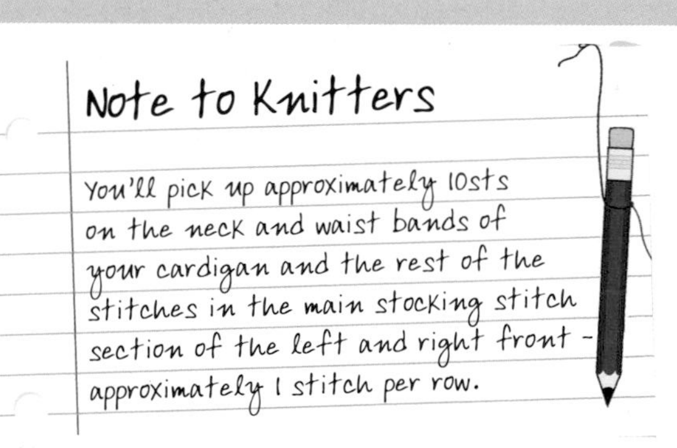

Note to Knitters

You'll pick up approximately 10sts on the neck and waist bands of your cardigan and the rest of the stitches in the main stocking stitch section of the left and right front - approximately 1 stitch per row.

Using 2.75mm needles and with RS facing, start at the top of the neck and pick up and knit 153 (165, 171, 183, 195)sts.

Row 1 (WS): P1, K1 rib to end (you'll start and end this row with a purl stitch).

Row 2 (RS): K1, P1 rib to end (you'll start and end this row with a knit stitch).

Repeat last 2 rows to a total of 10 rows, ending with a Row 2.

Cast off on WS of cardigan in pattern.

Right front button band

Using 2.75mm needles and with RS facing, starting at the waist of the cardigan, pick up and knit 153 (165, 171, 183, 195)sts.

Row 1 (WS): P1, K1 rib to end (you'll start and end this row with a purl stitch).

Row 2 (RS): K1, P1 rib to end (you'll start and end this row with a knit stitch).

Row 3 (WS): As Row 1.

Row 4 (RS): As Row 2.

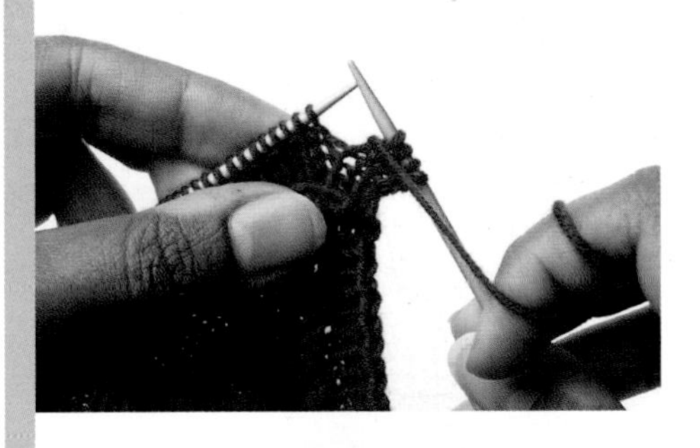

Row 5 (WS): P1, K1, P1, K1, YF, K2tog, [rib 12, YF, K2tog], repeat a further ten (11, 11, 12, 13) times, rib to end. You'll have a total of 11 (12, 12, 13, 14) buttonholes, which will appear after the next row of knitting.

Row 6 (RS): As Row 2 – look to see the buttonholes appearing and don't forget to count the stitches at the end of the row to make sure you still have the correct number.

Row 7 (WS): As Row 1.

Row 8 (RS): As Row 2.

Row 9 (WS): As Row 1.

Row 10 (RS): As Row 2.

Cast off on WS of cardigan in pattern.

Questions & Answers

What do you mean by 'rib 12'?

Before you work the buttonhole row, have a look at the Recognising rib workshop on p.40. 'Rib 12' means 'continue working 12sts in rib' – to do this you have to know which are the knit stitches and which are the purl stitches are simply by looking at them. Remember your V-necks and polo necks!

Note to Knitters

Your buttonholes might seem a bit small, but don't worry. Knitted buttonholes can stretch with use, so I've purposely made them small. Your 1cm buttons will squeeze in, and a tight fit means that they won't pop open (which I find a huge pain on some cardigans I own).

Handy HINT

Be patient with your finishing. On such a big project using fine yarn, a little extra care will really pay off. Consider the effort you put into making up your cardigan as a quarter of the total work you put into this project.

Sew sleeves

See how to sew a sleeve onto a body on p.33.

Sew the sleeves into the armhole opening. To get the best fit, fold the top of the sleeve in half to find the centre.

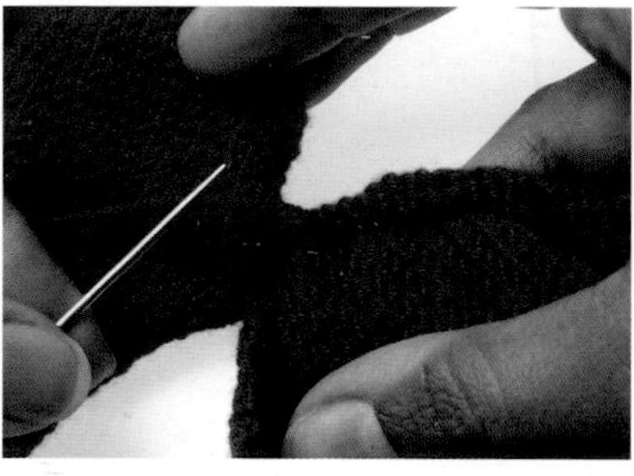

Start by sewing that to the shoulder seam. On the body, begin by finding the centre bar, and on the top of the sleeve you'll be looking for two sides of the 'V' (see p.33). Don't forget to ease in!

Work your way towards the underarm.

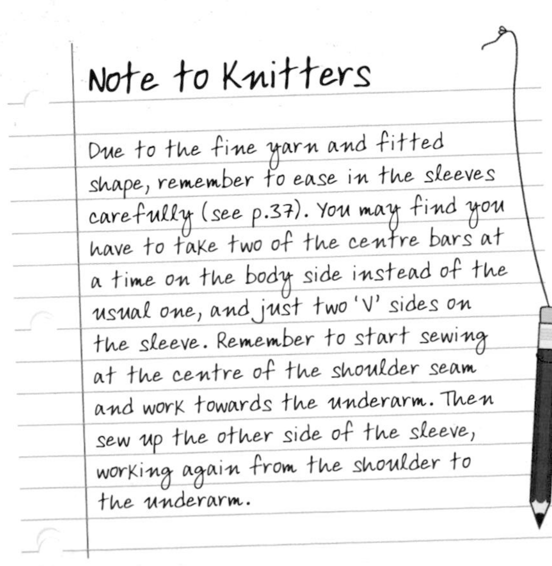

Note to Knitters

Due to the fine yarn and fitted shape, remember to ease in the sleeves carefully (see p.37). You may find you have to take two of the centre bars at a time on the body side instead of the usual one, and just two 'V' sides on the sleeve. Remember to start sewing at the centre of the shoulder seam and work towards the underarm. Then sew up the other side of the sleeve, working again from the shoulder to the underarm.

See Sewing-up workshop on p.32.

Sewing up something so finely knit and shaped means that you'll have to use your initiative – sometimes you'll

be picking up two sides of the 'V' and sometimes you'll be picking up the centre bar.

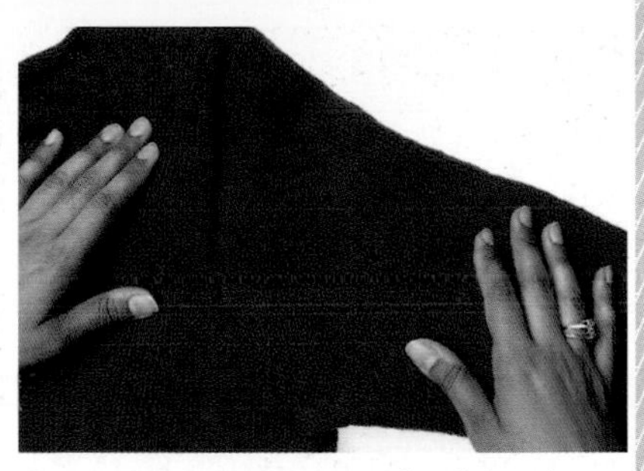

Once you've sewn one side of the sleeve to the body, you can go back to the middle, where you started sewing the sleeve to the body, and work your way down the other side.

Don't forget to keep an eye on the underarm – the start of the underarm decreasing is the point where the sleeve and the body must join up. You'll have to ease the sleeve in to make sure this happens.

Side and sleeve seams

Starting from the underarm, using 'centre-bar' mattress stitch, sew up from the underarm to the wrist, then

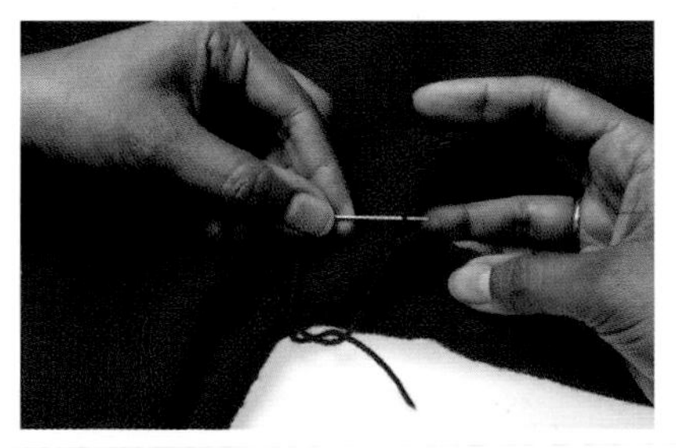

from the underarm to the waist of the cardigan.

Handy HINT

By starting the side and sleeve seams at the point of the underarm and working towards the wrist, then back from the point of the underarm to the waist of the cardigan, it ensures that you have an exact join between the sleeves and the body.

Buttons

Sew on the buttons securely – lay the cardigan flat, so you can match up the buttons with the buttonholes. When sewing on buttons, first sew the buttons at the top and the bottom of the cardigan, then the button in the middle, and then fill in the gaps. If you start sewing the buttons from one end and work your way along the button band, it's easy to make a mistake and run out of room for your buttons.

Weave in all your ends neatly.

PROJECT 7

Gloves

Gloves may seem fiddly little things to knit, but they make a perfect project if you'd like a knitting challenge but don't fancy a 'big' project.

You can add your own touches, using colours in any combination that strikes your fancy – maybe each finger in a different colour? Knitting gloves might seem like a project that needs a lot of coordination on your part, but once you get the hang of it, I reckon you'll be churning them out to make presents for everyone in no time. Don't forget to look at p.98 and knit a matching hat!

YOU WILL NEED

ANY STANDARD DOUBLE KNIT YARN, so you have lots of options when choosing
Ladies' gloves: 139m
Men's gloves: 154m

3MM KNITTING NEEDLES

3.75MM KNITTING NEEDLES

DARNING NEEDLE

Note to Knitters

Although the gauge is calculated using 4mm knitting needles, this pattern uses smaller needles than usual with double knit yarn. This is to create a tighter weave, so that the knitted fabric is warmer and denser. It will make nice, cosy gloves that will fend off winter wind chill.

GAUGE

24sts and 30 rows in stocking stitch, using 4mm needles = 10cm square.

SIZE

Ladies' gloves (men's gloves)

ABBREVIATIONS

K = Knit
P = Purl
St(s) = Stitch(es)
St st = Stocking stitch
1 x 1 rib = K1, P1 rib to end
K2tog = Knit two stitches together
M1 = Make one stitch by picking up the loop in between two stitches
Cont = Continue
Rep = Repeat
Rem = Remaining

START KNITTING

RIGHT HAND

Using 3mm needles, cast on 46 (52)sts.

Work 1 x 1 rib until piece measures 8 (6)cm from beginning.

Handy HINT

I suggest that if you alter the depth of the ribbed cuff, you also make a note of the number of rows you've knitted, using a tally. This means that when you knit the glove for the other hand, you can make sure it is exactly the same length.

Changing to 3.75mm needles and starting with a knit row, st st for 4 rows.

SHAPE THUMB GUSSET

K23 (25), M1, K3, M1, K to end. Count 48 (54) sts.

P 1 row.

K 1 row.

P 1 row.

K23 (25), M1, K5, M1, K to end. Count 50 (56)sts.

P 1 row.

K23 (25), M1, K7, M1, K to end. Count 52 (58)sts.

P 1 row.

K23 (25), M1, K9, M1, K to end. Count 54 (60)sts.

P 1 row.

K23 (25), M1, K11, M1, K to end. Count 56 (62)sts.

P 1 row.

K23 (25), M1, K13, M1, K to end. Count 58 (64)sts.

P 1 row.

Note to Knitters

Gloves that are too short are a pet hate of mine, as I get cold wrists. That's why I've knitted a longer cuff for the ladies' gloves than the men's, as I don't think gentlemen care as much about cold wrists as I do. However, if you want longer or shorter cuffs on the gloves, feel free to adjust the pattern with more or fewer rows of ribbing. Just remember that you'll need more yarn if you are increasing the ribbing.

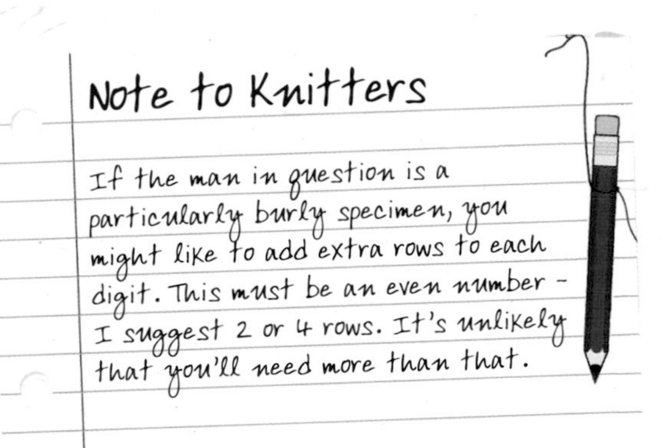

Note to Knitters

If the man in question is a particularly burly specimen, you might like to add extra rows to each digit. This must be an even number – I suggest 2 or 4 rows. It's unlikely that you'll need more than that.

You'll see your thumb gusset appearing.

For the longer-armed gent, you might like to add a few rows to the wristband to make a longer cuff.

Every time you cut the yarn whilst making these gloves, leave a long tail. This is so that you can weave in the ends using a darning needle rather than a crochet hook. It will make your life much easier the getting into the fiddly fingers when weaving in.

DIVIDE FOR THUMB

K38 (42)sts, turn (turning in the middle of a row means swapping the needles around in your hands, ready to start working in the other direction).

P15 (17)sts, turn.

Working on these 15 (17)sts only, st st a further 14 (18) rows on the thumb.

K2tog, rep to last stitch, K1. Count 8 (9)sts.

DRAWSTRING FINISH

Step 1: Thread the cut end of the yarn onto a darning needle.

Step 2: Pass the darning needle through the stitches remaining on the knitting needle, one by one, removing them from the knitting needle as they are secured by the yarn on the darning needle.

Step 3: Pull the yarn tight. The piece of knitting should now fall naturally into a thumb shape.

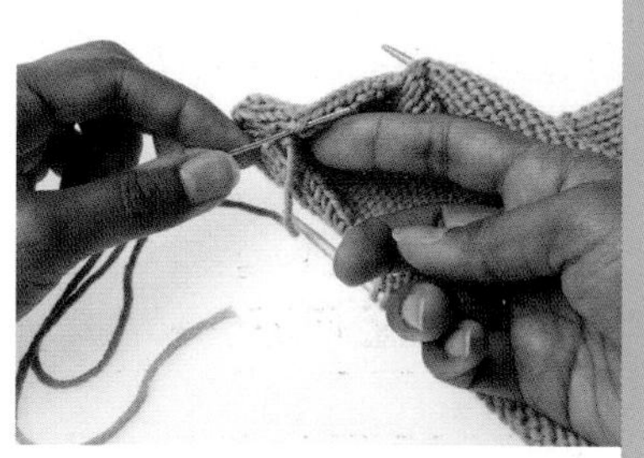

Sew up from the top of the thumb to the base, using mattress stitch.

All the sewing up for the gloves is done in side-to-side mattress stitch (see p.32) – picking up the centre bar inside the 'V' of the stitch.

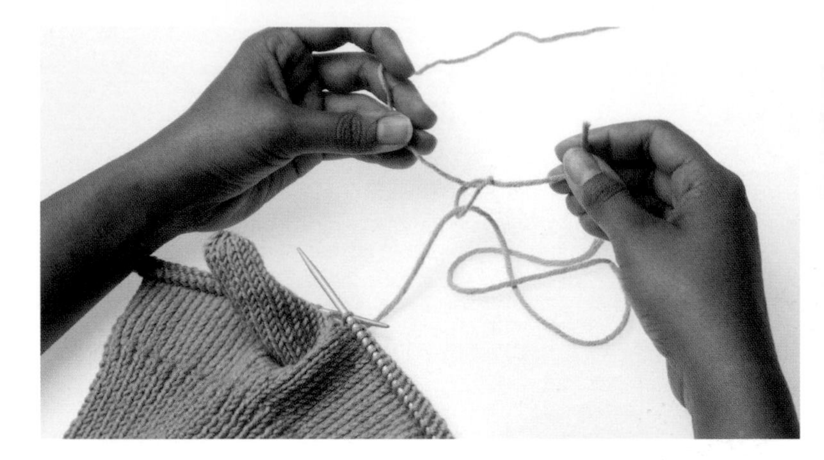

Join new yarn to the tail of yarn you've just sewn the thumb with, and with RS facing, knit to end.

HAND

Starting with a purl row, st st 11 (13) rows, ending with a purl row.

DIVIDE FOR FINGERS

FIRST FINGER

K28 (30), turn.

P13 (13), turn and cast on 2sts. Count 15 (15)sts.

Working on these 15 (15)sts only, st st a further 22 (24) rows, ending with a purl row.

K2tog, rep to last stitch, K1. Count 8 (8)sts.

Cut the yarn leaving a long tail (about 40cm), do a drawstring finish and sew up the finger from the tip to the base.

SECOND FINGER

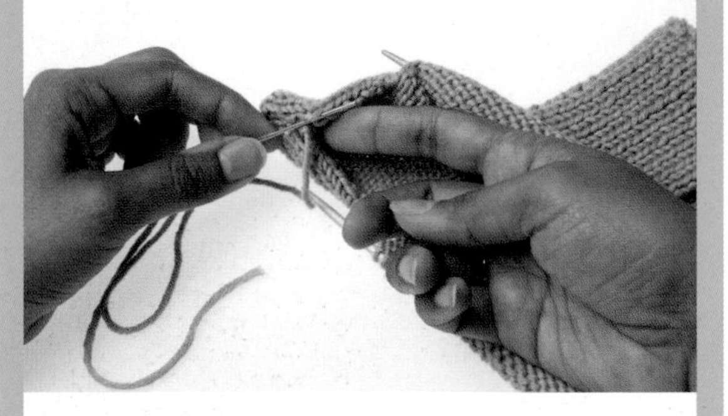

With RS facing, rejoin yarn to the yarn tail you've just sewn the first finger with, pick up and knit 2sts from the cast-on sts at the base of the first finger. K5 (6), turn.

P12 (14), turn and cast on 2sts. Count 14 (16)sts.

Working on these 14 (16)sts only, st st a further 24 (26) rows, ending with a purl row.

K2tog, rep to end. Count 7 (8)sts.

Cut the yarn, leaving a long tail (about 40cm), do a drawstring finish and sew up the finger from the tip to the base.

THIRD FINGER

With RS facing, rejoin yarn to the yarn tail you've just sewn the second finger with, pick up and knit 2sts from the cast-on sts at the base of the second finger.

K5 (6), turn.

P12 (14), turn and cast on 2sts. Count 14 (16)sts.

Working on these 14 (16)sts only, st st a further 20 (22) rows, ending with a purl row.

K2tog, rep to end. Count 7 (8)sts.

Cut the yarn leaving a long tail (about 40cm), do a drawstring finish and sew up the finger from the tip to the base.

LITTLE FINGER

With RS facing, rejoin yarn to the yarn tail you've just sewn the third finger with, pick up and knit 2sts from the cast-on sts at the base of the third finger.

K5 (5), turn.

P to end. Count 12 (12)sts.

Working on these 12 (12)sts only, st st a further 12 (14) rows, ending with a purl row.

K2tog, rep to end. Count 6 (6)sts.

Cut the yarn leaving a long tail (about 60cm), do a drawstring finish and sew up the finger and hand from the tip of the little finger to the beginning of the wrist.

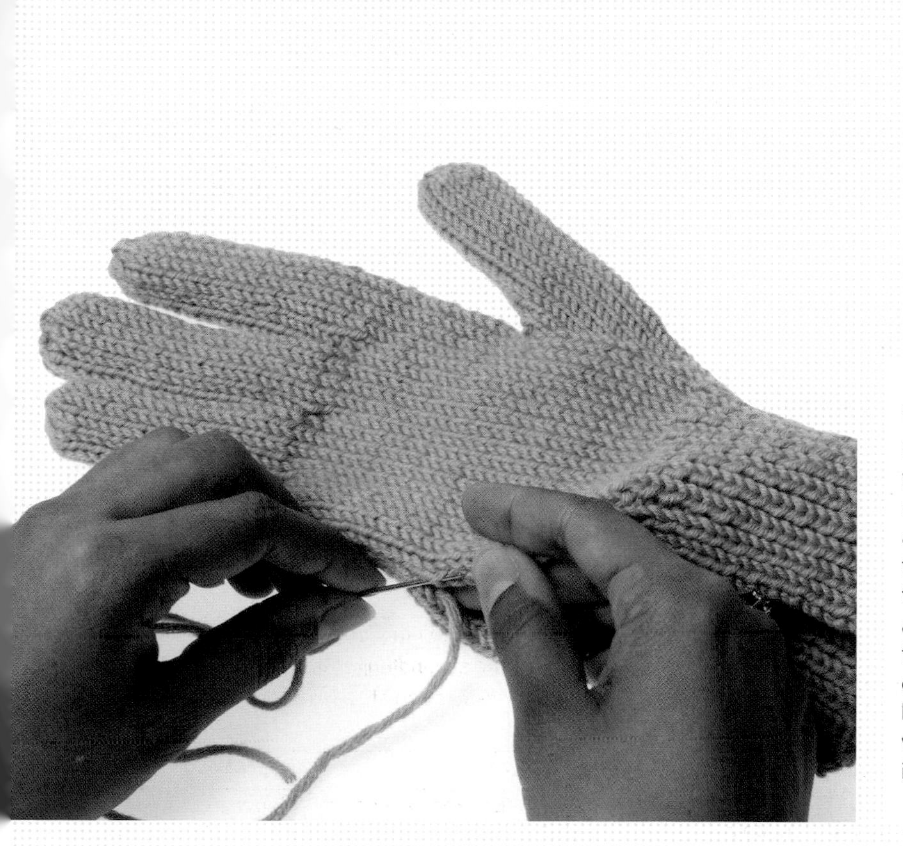

Weave in all your ends – remembering to use the weaving-in yarn on a darning needle to sew up, from the inside of the glove, any little holes you might find at the base of the digits. This is a fiddly job, but be patient (and have a snack before starting)! Take it from me that a tidy finish on a pair of gloves might take a bit of time, but will add much more in the way of 'oohs' and 'aahs' from your impressed friends.

Handy HINT

It is common to end up with little holes at the base of the thumb and fingers.

When you are weaving in the ends, you can use the tails of yarn at the base of the digits to sew up these holes from the inside of the glove.

Or if you find yarn is a bit bulky, you could use matching coloured sewing thread.

LEFT HAND

Using 3mm needles, cast on 46 (52)sts.

Work in 1 x 1 rib until piece measures 8 (6)cm from beginning.

Handy **HINT**

If you changed the depth of the ribbing on the right glove, remember to refer to your note of the number of rows you knitted, to make sure that you get exactly the same length on the left hand.

Change to 3.75mm needles and starting with a knit row, st st for 4 rows.

SHAPE THUMB GUSSET

K20 (22), M1, K3, M1, K to end. Count 48 (54)sts.

P 1 row.

K 1 row.

P 1 row.

K20 (22), M1, K5, M1, K to end. Count 50 (56)sts.

P 1 row.

K20 (22), M1, K7, M1, K to end. Count 52 (58)sts.

P 1 row.

K20 (22), M1, K9, M1, K to end. Count 54 (60)sts.

P 1 row.

K20 (22), M1, K11, M1, K to end. Count 56 (62)sts.

P 1 row.

K20 (22), M1, K13, M1, K to end. Count 58 (64)sts.

P 1 row.

DIVIDE FOR THUMB

K33 (39)sts, turn.

P15 (17)sts, turn.

Working on these 15 (17)sts only, st st a further 14 (18) rows on the thumb.

K2tog, rep to last stitch, K1. Count 8 (9)sts.

Do a drawstring finish.

Sew up from the top of the thumb to the base.

Join new yarn to the yarn tail you've just sewn the thumb with, and with RS facing, knit to end.

HAND

Starting with a purl row, st st 11 (13) rows, ending with a purl row.

DIVIDE FOR FINGERS

FIRST FINGER

K28 (30), turn.

P13 (13), turn and cast on 2sts. Count 15 (15)sts.

Working on these 15 (15)sts only, st st a further 22 (24) rows, ending with a purl row.

K2tog, rep to last stitch, K1. Count 8 (8)sts.

Cut the yarn leaving a long tail (about 40cm), do a drawstring finish and sew up the finger from the tip to the base.

SECOND FINGER

With RS facing, rejoin yarn to the yarn tail you've just sewn the first finger with, pick up and knit 2sts from the cast-on sts at the base of the first finger.

K5 (6), turn.

P12 (14), turn and cast on 2sts. Count 14 (16)sts.

Working on these 14 (16)sts only, st st a further 24 (26) rows, ending with a purl row.

K2tog, rep to end. Count 7 (8)sts.

Cut the yarn leaving a long tail (about 40cm), do a drawstring finish and sew up the finger from the tip to the base.

THIRD FINGER

With RS facing, rejoin yarn to the yarn tail you've just sewn the second finger with, pick up and knit 2sts from the cast-on sts at the base of the second finger.

K5 (6), turn.

P12 (14), turn and cast on 2sts. Count 14 (16)sts.

Working on these 14 (16)sts only, st st a further 20 (22) rows, ending with a purl row.

K2tog, rep to end. Count 7 (8)sts.

Cut the yarn leaving a long tail (about 40cm), do a drawstring finish and sew up the finger from the tip to the base.

LITTLE FINGER

With RS facing, rejoin yarn to the yarn tail you've just sewn the third finger with, pick up and knit 2sts from the cast-on sts at the base of the third finger.

K5 (5), turn.

P to end. Count 12 (12)sts.

Working on these 12 (12)sts only, st st a further 12 (14) rows, ending with a purl row.

K2tog, rep to end. Count 6 (6)sts.

Cut the yarn leaving a long tail (about 60cm), do a drawstring finish and sew up the finger and hand from the tip of the little finger to the beginning of the wrist.

Weave in all the ends - remembering to use the weaving-in yarn on a darning needle to sew up any little holes you might find at the base of the digits, from the inside of the glove.

Variations

You can personalise these gloves in many ways:

- Colour changes – you could even knit every digit in a different colour!
- Fingerless mitts – knit each digit to the length you want before casting off on the WS of the work and sewing up.
- Sew pretty things to the fingers or the back of the gloves, such as buttons or sequins, or embroidery.
- Adjust the length of the cuff – you could even lengthen it to reach as far as your elbow.

PROJECT 8

Hats: learn to knit in the round

Working in the round may seem like a very advanced knitting technique, but if you follow my few tips and tricks, I hope you'll soon be a convert to circular knitting.

Knitting in the round is traditionally used to knit socks on double-pointed needles, but these days, many knitters and designers take advantage of this seamless technique for all sorts of projects, including hats and even jumpers.

Circular knitting needles come in different lengths as well as needle sizes. The needle sizes are the same as with straight needles, it's the lengths that you'll need to think about in relation to your project. The length refers to the length of the needles taking into account the flexible part. For example, a 40cm circular needle is perfect for a hat. Any longer than that and the flexible part of the needle will be too long for the circumference of the knitting. If you want to knit anything smaller than a hat, for example where the crown of a hat narrows at the top of the head, or socks, you'll need to use double-pointed needles.

I'll start you off on circular needles for a hat and we'll move on to the instructions for double-pointed needles to finish the hat and then later to knit socks.

Handy **HINT**

If you would like a slightly bigger hat, or if your tension is quite tight, try using 5mm needles instead.

YOU WILL NEED

ANY STANDARD DOUBLE KNIT YARN
so you have lots of options when choosing. I hate an itchy hat on my forehead – bear in mind the person you are knitting for when you chose your yarn. For example, it's lovely to have the option of cotton when knitting for baby's sensitive skin – I love Debbie Bliss Eco Baby, which is an organic Fairtrade yarn in 100% cotton. Note that it's a little finer than a standard double knit yarn, so the hat may turn out to be a little bit smaller.
Baby: 51m
Child: 60m
Adult small: 84m
Adult large: 108m

4MM KNITTING NEEDLES

4MM CIRCULAR NEEDLES, 40CM LONG

4MM DOUBLE-POINTED NEEDLES, 20CM LONG

DARNING NEEDLE

Note to Knitters

These yarn requirements are approximate since your tension may vary as you are learning to knit in the round.

GAUGE

22sts and 30 rows in stocking stitch, using 4mm needles = 10cm square.

SIZE

Baby (child, adult small, adult large)

The hat can be knitted in four sizes, approximate to the age/size of the wearer. The fit of the child size will depend on the age of the child; you can make the 'adult small' size for an older child. The main pattern instructions are for a hat with a rolled brim; instructions for a hat with a ribbed border are given separately.

ABBREVIATIONS

K = Knit

P = Purl

St(s) = Stitch(es)

St st = Stocking stitch (remember that this is K 1 row, P 1 row on straight needles, and K every round if you are working in the round)

1 x 1 rib = K1, P1 rib to end

K2tog = Knit two stitches together

Dpn(s) = Double-pointed needle(s)

Rep = Repeat

START KNITTING

Using 4mm straight needles and leaving a long tail of yarn (about 20cm), cast on 66 (77, 88, 99)sts.

Starting with a knit row, work in st st for 4 rows, ending on a purl row.

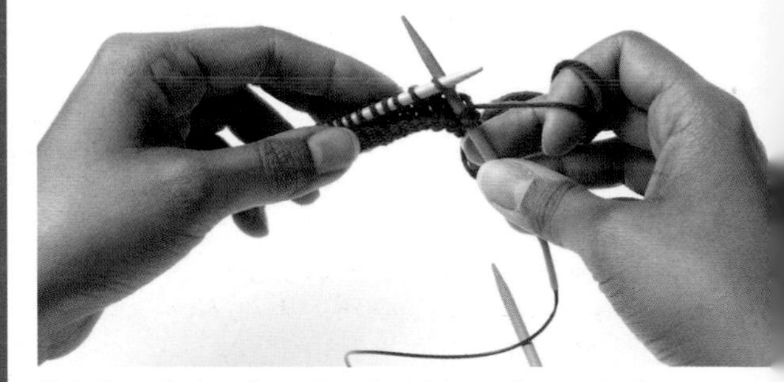

Knit the stitches from the straight needles on to the 4mm circular needle.

Note to Knitters

Using straight needles to start a piece of knitting in the round isn't the most traditional way of working, but if you don't have an expert to help you, it is a way of guaranteeing that your work will not get twisted when you join (which is a huge pain). I still sometimes use this technique myself – there's never any harm in making life a little easier. When you get to the end of your work, the little gap at the beginning that you knitted on straight needles can be sewn up easily for a tidy finish.

Ribbed border variation

The main pattern shown with the images will produce a hat with a rolled stocking stitch brim. For a ribbed border, you'll have to follow the slightly different pattern – shown here – but the technique for joining into the round is the same.

Baby and adult small sizes (an even number of cast-on stitches):

- Using straight 4mm needles, cast on 66 (88)sts.
- Work 1 x 1 rib to end.
- Rep the last row a further three times to make a total of 4 rows of rib.
- Work in 1 x 1 rib and transfer the stitches on to a circular needle or three double-pointed needles (distributed equally).

Once the stitches are all on the circular needles, you'll notice that the knitting is probably twisted along the flexible part of the needle.

Carefully spread out the stitches so that they are untwisted. Keep the working end of the yarn on the right-hand side.

Next you'll need a stitch marker. You can buy these, or (as I prefer to do) use a piece of contrasting coloured yarn tied in a slip knot, which works just as well.

Place the marker on the tip of the right-hand needle, just on top of the last worked stitch. The working yarn is now on the right-hand needle.

Taking care that you haven't twisted the knitting - so it remains a true circle - knit the first stitch from the left part of the circular needle on to the right part of the circular needle. Keep knitting until you get back round to the stitch marker. You have now knitted one round.

- Place marker and join into the round taking care not to twist (follow the instructions with the images for how to do this).
- Note: the first stitch after the marker is a knit stitch. Therefore you'll start every round with a knit and end with a purl just before the marker.
- When you have a total of 4cm of rib, knit every round (this will create stocking stitch in the round) and follow the main pattern to the end.

Hat with ribbed border for child and adult large (an odd number of cast-on stitches):

- Using straight 4mm needles, cast on 77 (99)sts.
- Row 1: K1, P1 rib to end (you'll start and end this row with a knit stitch).
- Row 2: P1, K1 rib to end (you'll start and end this row with a purl stitch).
- Row 3: As Row 1.
- Starting and ending with a purl stitch, work in 1 x 1 rib and transfer the stitches on to a circular needle or three double-pointed needles (distributed equally).
- Place marker and join into the round taking care not to twist (follow the instructions with images on how to do this) – when you join into a round, the first joining stitch will be a purl stitch.
- Note that the stitch either side of the marker will be a purl stitch. That means you'll have two purls next to each other on the rib. Don't worry, as this won't stand out on the rib, and will make it much easier to follow the rest of the pattern after the ribbed border.
- When you have a total of 4cm of rib, knit every round (this will create stocking stitch in the round) and follow the main pattern to the end.

Note to Knitters

Working back and forth on straight needles is called making ROWS. When working on circular or double-pointed needles, you are making ROUNDS. In the round, you create stocking stitch by knitting every round. There is no need to purl. This is because you are essentially always on the right side of your work. Clever, eh?!

The most important rule when working in the round is that the yarn should always be in your right hand, even when you pick up your knitting. If you find that the yarn is in your left hand, STOP and turn your work!

At the end of the round, you'll reach the marker. Slip this without knitting it.

At the end of your first round, you may see a short line of yarn where you made the initial join into the round. Keep knitting, pulling a little tighter at the join for the first couple of rounds, and that will disappear.

After knitting the first round, check again to be sure that the knitting hasn't twisted.

If you check carefully for the first 3 or 4 rounds that there is no twisting, you're home and dry, as the shape of the hat will be set and unable to twist.

After a few rounds, you'll see that the knitting is joining together seamlessly. There will be a small gap where you knitted on straight needles in the beginning, but you can easily sew this up later, using the length of yarn you left at the cast-on edge for this purpose.

Handy HINT

Pull tighter for the first couple of stitches at the beginning of every round. This will ensure a seamless join. And don't worry if you can see the join - this can take a bit of practice to get right. Also, remember to slip the marker every time.

Handy HINT

When putting away your knitting in the round, push the stitches away from the tips to the flexible part of the needle. This will prevent the stitches from falling off the needles when you aren't knitting.

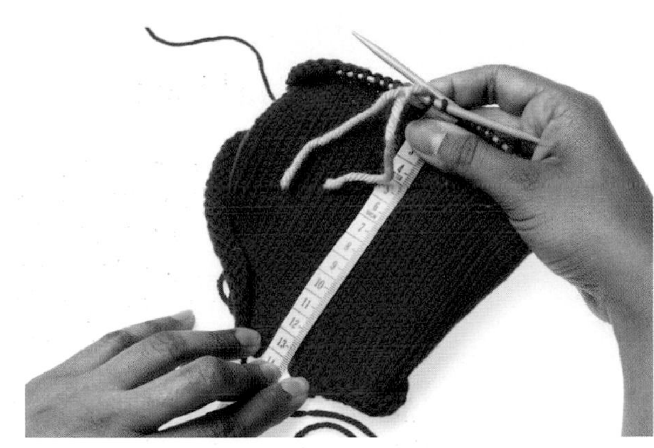

One of the joys of knitting in the round is seeing your work magically appear fully formed, with very little sewing up to do.

Knitting every round, continue in st st until the piece measures 13 (15, 17, 19)cm from the beginning.

DECREASE FOR TOP OF HAT (changing over to double-pointed needles as the circumference of your hat gets smaller)
BABY
[K4, K2tog], repeat to end. Count 55sts.
[K3, K2tog], repeat to end. Count 44sts.
[K2, K2tog], repeat to end. Count 33sts.
[K1, K2tog], repeat to end. Count 22sts.
[K2tog], repeat to end. Count 11sts.
CHILD
[K5, K2tog], repeat to end. Count 66sts.
- then follow instructions for baby.
ADULT SMALL
[K6, K2tog], repeat to end. Count 77sts.
[K5, K2tog], repeat to end. Count 66sts.
- then follow instructions for baby.
ADULT LARGE
[K7, K2tog], repeat to end. Count 88sts.
[K6, K2tog], repeat to end. Count 77sts.
[K5, K2tog], repeat to end. Count 66sts.
- then follow instructions for baby.

Note to Knitters

As you get fewer and fewer stitches, you will need to work the stitches equally onto three double-pointed needles. This is so that you have enough room to work as the stitches get closer together and the circular needle becomes too long. I suggest that you change to double-pointed needles after the first decrease round on the baby's hat and the second decrease round on the bigger sizes.

Changing over to double-pointed needles

You'll notice, as you work these decreases, that eventually the circular needle becomes too long as the stitches get fewer and fewer. When this happens, work the next round (continuing the decreases as shown on the pattern) by knitting approximately one-third of the stitches on to one of the double-pointed needles (dpns). You'll need to do this after the first or second set of decreases.

Then push the stitches you've just knitted to the centre of the dpn (they'll stay there quite happily for now) and work the next third of the stitches on to another dpn.

You now have two-thirds of the stitches on two dpns and one-third still on the circular needle.

Knit the remaining stitches from the circular needle on to a third dpn (remembering to work the decreases at the same time). Well done! I know this part is fiddly!

Handy HINT

If the marker falls off once you start knitting on double-pointed needles, don't worry. It's the join where you can see the cast-on tail of yarn that's the start and finish of each round.

To work in the round on double-pointed needles, you start knitting on to a fourth double-pointed needle. When you've worked the stitches from one needle, you'll be left with an empty needle. You then use that to work the stitches on the next needle. Each time you work a needle, you'll be left with an empty needle on which to knit the next stitches. Don't panic – this will make sense when you do it!

Now continue working the pattern in the round on the dpns. This will seem strange at first, but persevere! A student once described it as knitting into a bird's nest, and you will get poked by the needles a few times, but my advice is to simply squash the stitches on the needles you aren't using to the middle of the needles and ignore them. They won't slip off: they'll just hang in there, waiting for their turn.

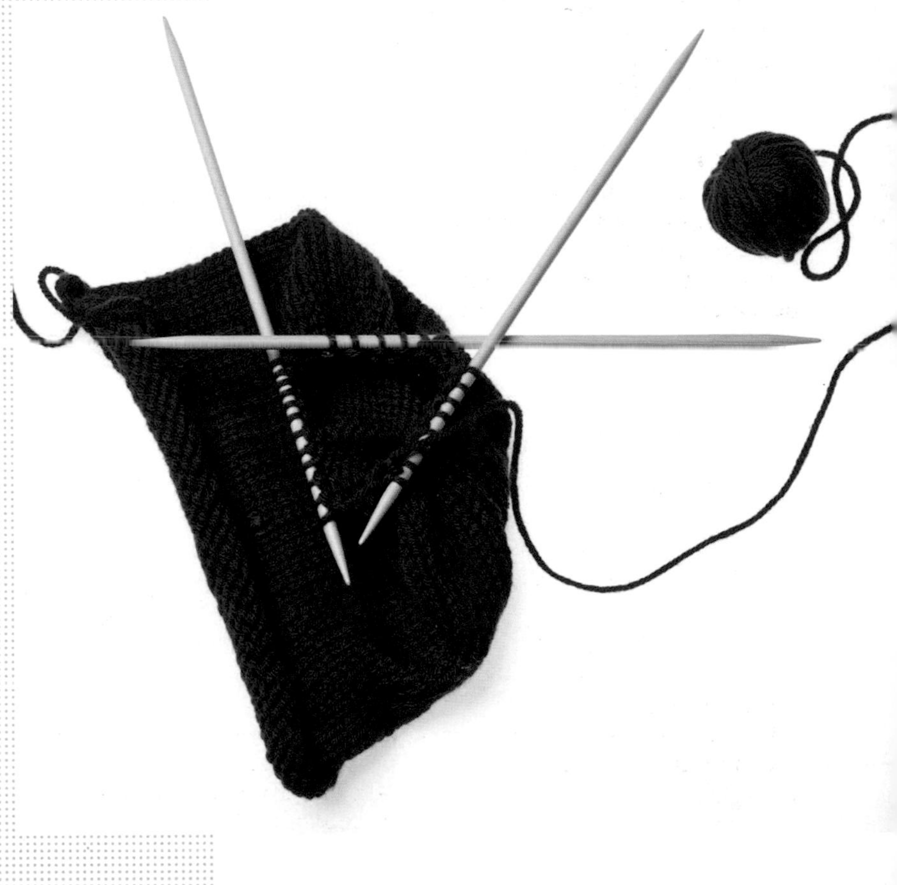

As the stitches get fewer and fewer as you decrease towards the crown of the hat, the double-pointed needles move closer and closer together to make a smaller triangle. Circular needles wouldn't be able to do this, which is why we need to transfer the hat stitches to double-pointed needles.

Finishing

There are a couple of ways to do this. The simplest way is to work a drawstring finish.

Cut the yarn, leaving a long tail. Thread the end onto a darning needle, and pass the stitches from the dpns on to the darning needle.

Pull the drawstring tightly to close the opening at the top of the hat.

On the inside of the hat, weave this end in using small stitches sewn around the hole at the top of the hat.

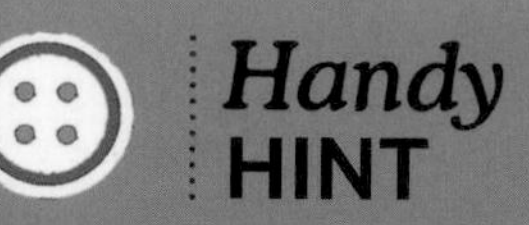

This is a pretty simple hat pattern, but you can think creatively and add a different border, use colourwork (see p.164), Swiss darning (see p.170), or simply sew on buttons or sequins to create any unique look you like.

Making up

Sew up the small opening at the beginning of the hat where you worked on straight needles. You'll have left a 20cm length of yarn for this.

Weave in all your ends.

If you are making one of the smaller sizes (or indeed any size you like), I-cord (see p.28) makes an adorable alternative finish. When you've completed the decreases, transfer the final 11sts onto a double-pointed needle and work your I-cord. This looks particularly cute on the baby size – you could even sew a pompom onto the end of your I-cord.

Workshop: *Using double-pointed needles*

For circular knitting projects, you can knit in the round directly on double-pointed needles (dpns) without using circular needles at all.

You need this technique for socks, but it works just as well on hats if you find you prefer dpns to circular needles.

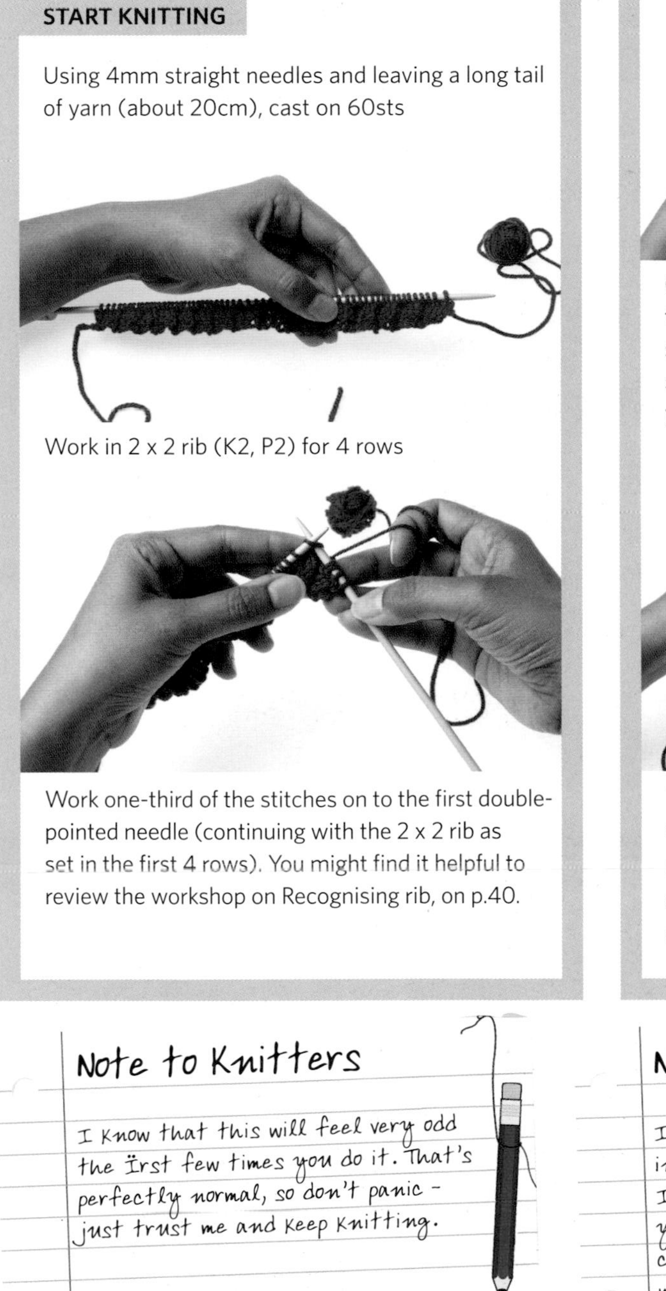

START KNITTING

Using 4mm straight needles and leaving a long tail of yarn (about 20cm), cast on 60sts

Work in 2 x 2 rib (K2, P2) for 4 rows

Work one-third of the stitches on to the first double-pointed needle (continuing with the 2 x 2 rib as set in the first 4 rows). You might find it helpful to review the workshop on Recognising rib, on p.40.

Once you've done that, squash those stitches to the centre of the first dpn – this will hold the stitches on the needle as you start using the second dpn, keeping the first lot of stitches out of your way.

Take a second dpn and work the next third of the stitches on to it.

Once you have worked the next third of the stitches on to the second dpn, squash those stitches to the middle as well.

Note to Knitters

I know that this will feel very odd the first few times you do it. That's perfectly normal, so don't panic – just trust me and keep knitting.

Note to Knitters

I've used the same number of cast-on stitches in the images above as for the Ladies' sock, but I've done the workshop photos on double knit yarn and 4mm needles, so you can see it more clearly than on skinny sock yarn. Use this workshop with the sock materials and cast-on numbers when you are knitting your socks.

Finally, work the remaining stitches from the straight needle onto a third dpn.

Now to join!

Once all the stitches are on the three dpns, you'll notice that the stitches are all twisted about the needles.

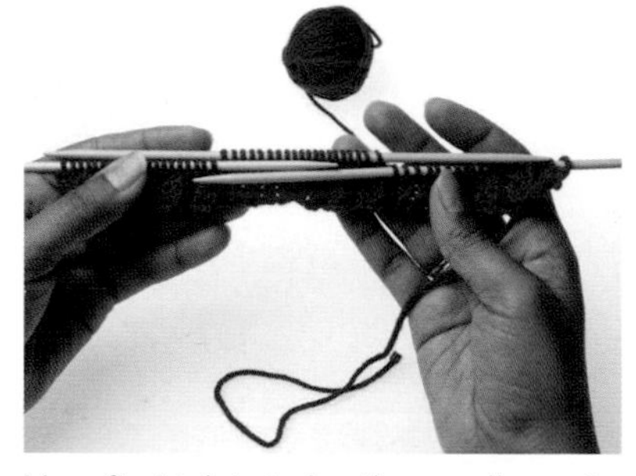

Your first job is to lay the needles out flat and straighten up the stitches. Keep the working end of the yarn on the right-hand side. Take extra care to ensure that the stitches aren't twisted around the needles, especially at the point where the needles meet. It's here that it's easy to make a mistake, so really take your time.

Fold the needles closed so they form a triangle.

Work a couple of stitches to close the triangle.

Next, take a fourth (new) double-pointed needle and work the stitches from the first dpn on to the empty needle.

Handy HINT

Once again, I know this feels odd, but keep the stitches on the needles you aren't currently working from squished to the middle of each needle, so they are out of your way, and simply ignore them. Easier said than done, you might say, as they can poke you, but persevere!

Keep knitting your ribbed border. Each time you work the stitches on to an empty double-pointed needle, you'll end up with a new empty needle. Put that empty dpn into your right hand and work the stitches from the next needle on to it.

What you are doing now is working in ROUNDS.

As with the instructions for starting on a circular needle, when you finish the first round, lay out the work to check you haven't twisted it. These twists can easily happen in the first few rounds - the place to check is where each needle meets the one next to it. After you've worked a few rounds, the work will be set in its round and you won't need to keep checking it. Don't worry if there's a strand of yarn at the join after the first round: it will disappear after you've worked a couple more rounds.

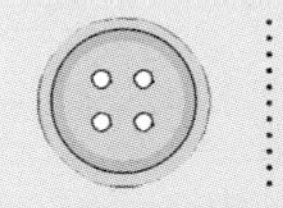

Handy HINT

The most important rule, when working in the round, is that the yarn should always be in your right hand, even when you pick up your knitting. If you find that the yarn is in your left hand, STOP and turn your work.

Questions & Answers

Panic! I've worked my first round and it looks like the work has twisted!

If this happens in the first round, you can untwist your work by rearranging the needles at the point where they meet the next needle. You can only correct this in the first couple of rounds, which is why it's so important to check.

This technique of using double-pointed needles works on most knitting in the round; you'll definitely need it for knitting socks. If you are a bit nervous, I suggest that you knit the hat before attempting socks, as the socks use much finer yarn and needles, so everything's just that little bit more fiddly. It's not essential of course – feel free to be brave and dive into sock knitting straight away: you can always undo your work and try again if you aren't happy. That's one of the joys of knitting!

PROJECT 9

Socks

Socks can seem like the holy grail of knitting. My students often tell me that their long-term knitting goal is to knit socks and the main question I hear is: 'Aren't socks *reeeally* difficult?'

My answer is always the same – nothing is difficult if you approach it at the right time and if it's explained in bite-sized pieces. By the 'right time', I mean that you'll enjoy knitting socks more if you are confident with the core skills of knitting. It is a good idea to have several small and large projects under your belt first, so that the basics of casting on, knitting and ribbing will already be second nature and you can concentrate on learning the new skills required for socks.

You might also like to knit a basic hat in the round (see p.98) to hone your circular knitting skills before you start working on tiny double-pointed needles for 4-ply socks. As for the 'bite-sized pieces', I've broken the pattern right down into simple stages with images, so sock knitting won't feel like a risky adventure, but rather an achievable challenge. You'll find plenty of support, hints and tips in my step-by-step instructions.

Before you embark on knitting socks, ask yourself:

1. Can I recognise rib stitches? (See p.40.)
2. Have I knitted the hat pattern in the round? (See p.98.)
3. Can I pick up and knit? (See p.29.)

If the answer to all the above is yes, then you are ready for socks!

Handy HINT

If you've never knitted in the round or on double-pointed needles, I suggest that you have a go at knitting a hat in the round first, as that uses 4mm needles and double knit yarn, which is less fiddly when you're learning a new technique than the fine needles and yarn used in this sock pattern.

Socks can be knitted in any weight of yarn, but my favourite socks, and the ones I find the most satisfying to make, are fine-knit socks in 4-ply sock yarn. These are lightweight enough to wear with shoes (as opposed to chunky slipper socks), and make a great little project to take with you when you travel, as you don't have to carry huge amounts of materials.

I suggest that you always use proper sock yarn (for the adults' sizes), as the yarn includes a small amount of man-made fibre to add strength. Remember that socks are subjected to a lot more wear and tear than most knitted garments, especially around the heel, and you don't want to spend ages knitting something that will end up in tatters after a few wears. That would be very disheartening! For babies' socks, you can use any 4-ply yarn, as these will get less wear than adults' socks.

All in all, sock knitting is a nifty skill for a knitter to have; it's very hard not to get addicted, and socks make lovely gifts to impress your friends and family with … and for yourself, of course!

Note to Knitters

Beware of succumbing to the one-sock syndrome! It's easy to knit one sock and forget about knitting another. Unless you are a one-legged pirate, get knitting that second sock as soon as you finish the first one. Alternatively, you could get a second set of double-pointed needles and knit both socks at the same time.

GAUGE

Approximately 28sts and 40 rows in stocking stitch, using 2.25mm needles = 10cm square.

SIZE

Babies/toddlers (ladies, men)
This pattern is for an average-sized foot. Don't worry, as you can adjust the length later in the pattern depending on your shoe size. Please note that all the images relate to the ladies' size, but the techniques are the same for all sizes.

ABBREVIATIONS

K = Knit

P = Purl

2 x 2 rib = K2, P2 rib to end

St(s) = Stitch(es)

Sl = Slip a stitch from one needle to the next without knitting it

K2tog = Knit two stitches together

SSK = Slip, slip, knit

Dpn(s) = Double-pointed needle(s)

Knitwise = Treat stitches as if you were about to knit them

Purlwise = Treat stitches as if you were about to purl them

YOU WILL NEED

LOOK FOR SPECIALIST SOCK YARNS, for example Regia, Opal, Araucania Ranco and Mini Mochi. Using a sock-specific yarn will ensure that the socks wear well.
Babies'/toddlers' socks: 72m
Ladies' socks: 300m
Men's socks: 335m

2.5MM DOUBLE-POINTED KNITTING NEEDLES, 15–20CM LONG

3.5MM STRAIGHT KNITTING NEEDLES

CROCHET HOOK
I suggest using a tiny 2mm hook for the pick-up and knit at the heel

DARNING NEEDLE

Handy HINT

If you are using a self-patterning yarn, try to make sure that you start knitting the second sock at the same point in the colour repeat as the first sock. It'll make a subtle difference and give your socks a more professional look.

Note to Knitters

Of course, if you are knitting for larger than average feet, you'll need more yarn. I always think it's best to buy more yarn rather than less, and you can always knit a couple of pairs of the children's socks if you have any yarn left over.

Note to Knitters

This pattern features my easy technique of using straight needles for the cast-on and then moving on to double-pointed needles. Alternatively, feel free to cast on directly to the double-pointed needles if you are experienced at using them – but do take care not to twist when you join into the round.

START KNITTING

CUFF

Using the straight 3.5mm knitting needles, and leaving a long tail of yarn about 30cm long, cast on 36 (60, 72)sts.

Work in 2 x 2 rib for 4 rows.

Transfer the 2 x 2 rib sts, as equally as possible, onto three 2.5mm dpns.

Join into a round with the first 2sts, BEING VERY CAREFUL NOT TO TWIST THE STITCHES. See the workshop on knitting in the round on double-pointed needles (p.107) if you need a reminder.

The cast-on tail of yarn shows the beginning of the round.

Work in 2 x 2 rib until piece measures 3 (7, 8)cm from the beginning.

Note to Knitters

Don't forget that you are now knitting ROUNDS as opposed to ROWS. This is important to remember later in the pattern, when you start knitting the heel.

Remember to check your knitting for twisting at the end of every round for the first few rounds.

***Handy* HINT**

This can seem fiddly, working on such fine yarn and double-pointed needles, but many intermediate knitters have tested these instructions for me and most think that if you take your time, persevere and don't give up, knitting socks on double-pointed needles is achievable!

***Handy* HINT**

See p.40 for how to recognise rib stitches – it will make your life much easier when ribbing in the round on such fine yarn.

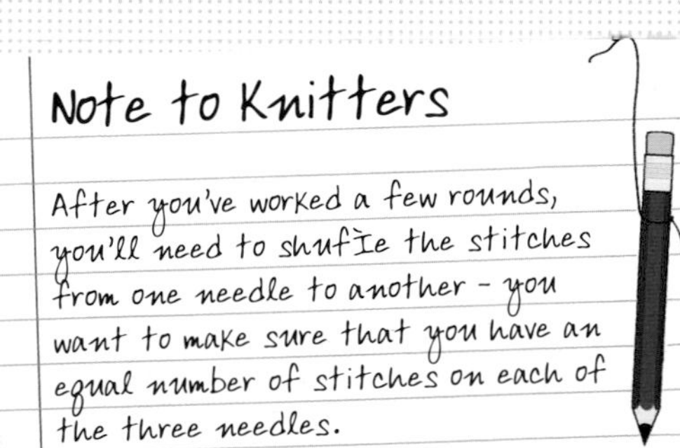

Note to Knitters

Needle one is the first needle after the cast-on tail; this makes the next one needle two, and the needle just before the cast-on tail needle three.

Questions & Answers

I seem to have a ladder running down my socks where the double-pointed needles meet, but I haven't dropped a stitch. What's going on?

That's a standard feature of a beginner's sock. It's where you've pulled too tightly on the first stitch between the needles, and it's unlikely to disappear when wearing the sock. I find that if I'm too tense when knitting on dpns, I get that 'ladder' on the side, too. In your next sock, try to relax a bit and don't pull too tightly when you move from one needle to the next. I know that's counter-intuitive, but trust me! After a bit more experience with double-pointed needles, this will stop happening.

LEG

Knit every round (on dpns this creates stocking stitch without needing to purl) until the piece measures 7 (21, 22)cm from the beginning. Be sure to work until the end of the round – the cast-on yarn tail will show you where this is.

Slip knit stitches knitwise, and slip purl stitches purlwise.

Note to Knitters

So far, you've been knitting in the round. For the heel Iap, you will be knitting and purling in ROWS, because you are now working as for straight knitting rather than knitting in the round.

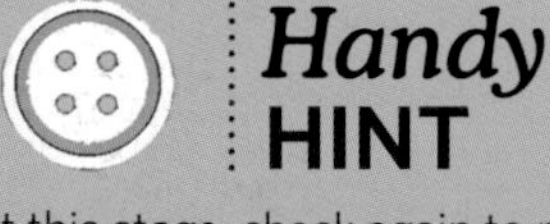

At this stage, check again to make sure you have 12 (20, 24)sts on each needle.

HEEL FLAP

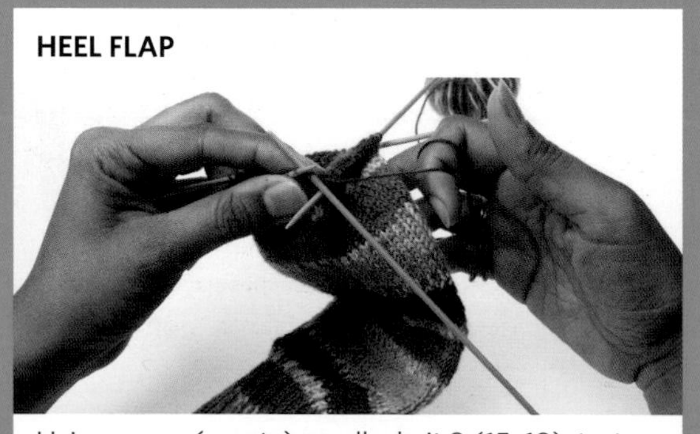

Using a new (empty) needle, knit 9 (15, 18)sts, turn.

Slip one st, P17 (29, 35)sts – 8 (14, 17) from the first needle and 9 (15, 18) from the second needle. When you start knitting the stitches from the second needle, you'll be working with only three needles (knitting on to the new needle), so it might feel a bit awkward.

Most of the stitches are now on one needle. Turn.

Using another new needle:

Row 1: Slip one st, K17 (29, 35), turn

The stitches are now on four needles.

The 18 (30, 36) heel-flap stitches are now all on the same needle.

At this stage, it makes it easier to work if you transfer (without knitting) the non-heel stitches equally on to two needles, discarding the fourth needle so the sock is once again on three needles.

You now have 9 (15, 18) stitches on two needles, and 18 (30, 36) stitches on the heel-flap needle.

You will now ignore the non-heel stitches and work only on the 18 (30, 36) heel-flap stitches.

Row 2: Slip 1, P17 (29, 35), turn.

Work the last 2 rows a further 8 (14, 17) times EACH.

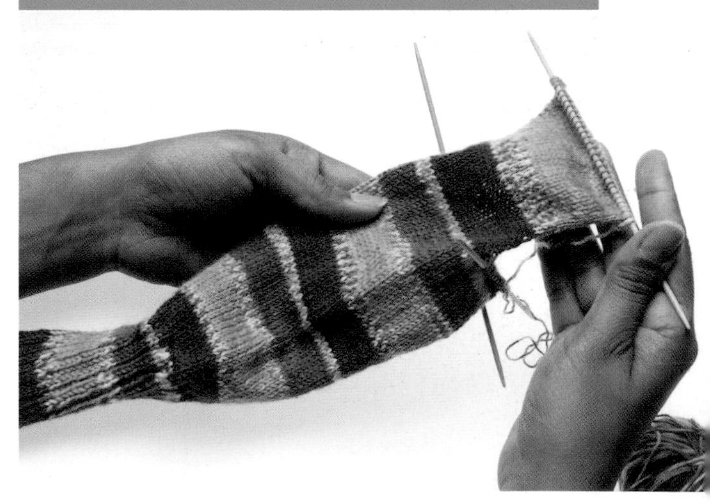

This is what the heel flap will look like.

The following charts might help you knit your heel flap – cross off the rows as you work them.

Babies'/toddlers' socks	
Row 1	Row 2
Sl1, K15.	Sl1, P15.
Sl1, K15.	Sl1, P15.
Sl1, K15.	Sl1, P15.
Sl1, K15.	Sl1, P15.
Sl1, K15.	Sl1, P15.
Sl1, K15.	Sl1, P15.
Sl1, K15.	Sl1, P15.
Sl1, K15.	Sl1, P15.

Ladies' socks	
Row 1	Row 2
Sl1, K29.	Sl1, P29.
Sl1, K29.	Sl1, P29.
Sl1, K29.	Sl1, P29.
Sl1, K29.	Sl1, P29.
Sl1, K29.	Sl1, P29.
Sl1, K29.	Sl1, P29.
Sl1, K29.	Sl1, P29.
Sl1, K29.	Sl1, P29.
Sl1, K29.	Sl1, P29.
Sl1, K29.	Sl1, P29.
Sl1, K29.	Sl1, P29.
Sl1, K29.	Sl1, P29.
Sl1, K29.	Sl1, P29.
Sl1, K29.	Sl1, P29.

Men's socks	
Row 1	Row 2
Sl1, K35.	Sl1, P35.
Sl1, K35.	Sl1, P35.
Sl1, K35.	Sl1, P35.
Sl1, K35.	Sl1, P35.
Sl1, K35.	Sl1, P35.
Sl1, K35.	Sl1, P35.
Sl1, K35.	Sl1, P35.
Sl1, K35.	Sl1, P35.
Sl1, K35.	Sl1, P35.
Sl1, K35.	Sl1, P35.
Sl1, K35.	Sl1, P35.
Sl1, K35.	Sl1, P35.
Sl1, K35.	Sl1, P35.
Sl1, K35.	Sl1, P35.
Sl1, K35.	Sl1, P35.
Sl1, K35.	Sl1, P35.
Sl1, K35.	Sl1, P35.
Sl1, K35.	Sl1, P35.

HEEL

You will now turn the heel (this decreases the stitches on the heel flap).

With the RS of the work facing you and working on the 18 (30, 36) heel sts:

K11 (17, 20), SSK, K1, turn.

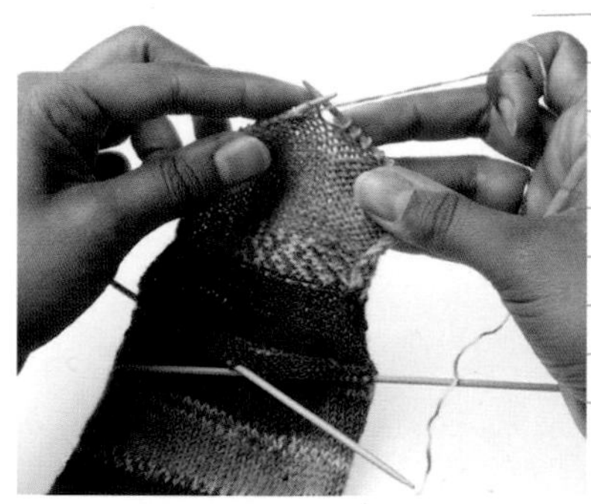

P6 (6, 5), P2tog, P1, turn.

Knit to last stitch before the gap – i.e. K7 (7, 6)sts, SSK (slip one st from either side of the gap for this SSK), K1, turn.

Note to Knitters

Where you turned, you'll see there is a gap in the stitches. You SSK or P2tog either side of this gap.

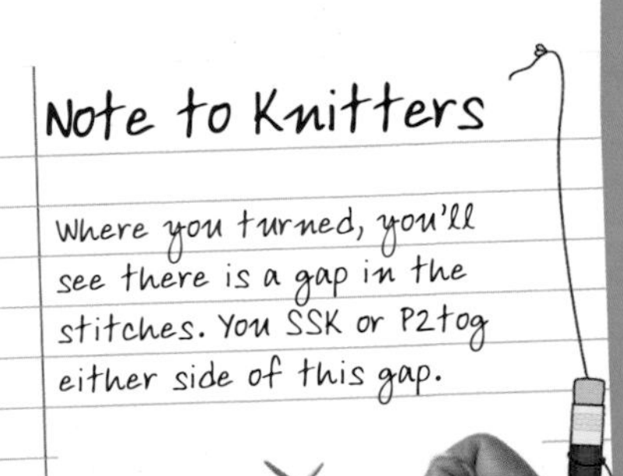

Purl to last stitch before the gap – i.e. P8 (8, 7)sts, P2tog (P2tog from either side of the gap for this P2tog), P1, turn.

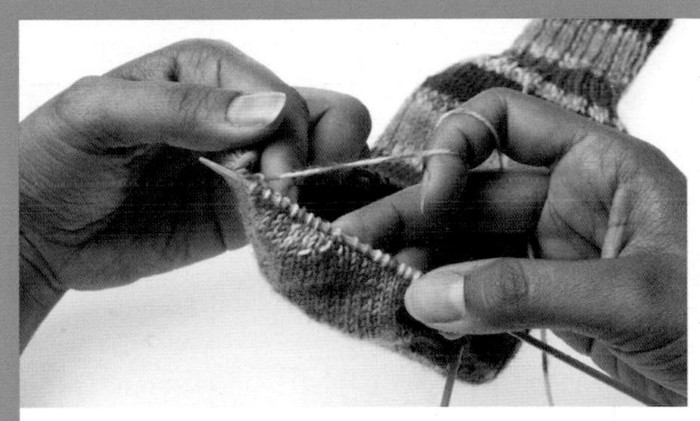

You'll see the heel start to emerge as you work the shaping rows.

Repeat the last 2 rows until 12 (18, 20)sts remain on the heel section.

Use the chart (right) to tick off the rows as you work them.

Babies'/toddlers' socks	Men's socks
K9, SSK, K1, turn.	K8, SSK, K1, turn.
P9, P2tog, P1, turn.	P9, P2tog, P1, turn.
	K10, SSK, K1, turn.
Ladies' socks	P11, P2tog, P1, turn.
K9, SSK, K1, turn.	K12, SSK, K1, turn.
P10, P2tog, P1, turn.	P13, P2tog, P1, turn.
K11, SSK, K1, turn.	K14, SSK, K1, turn.
P12, P2tog, P1, turn.	P15, P2tog, P1, turn.
K13, SSK, K1, turn.	K16, SSK, K1, turn.
P14, P2tog, P1, turn.	P17, P2tog, P1, turn.
K15, SSK, K1, turn.	K18, SSK, turn.
P16, P2tog, P1, turn.	P19, P2tog, turn.

Count 12 (18, 20)sts. This is needle one.

K 1 row.

Now you will pick up and knit the heel – you will be picking up and knitting the stitches you slipped when you were knitting and purling the heel-flap rows.

Hold the sock so that the knit side of the work is facing you.

Needle one: Using needle one (the needle that the heel stitches are on) and your crochet hook, pick up and knit 9 (15, 18)sts.

Use the slipped stitches as a guide – they will look like long stitches at the very edge of the heel flap. If you slipped correctly when knitting the heel flap, you should have the exact amount of stitches to pick up.

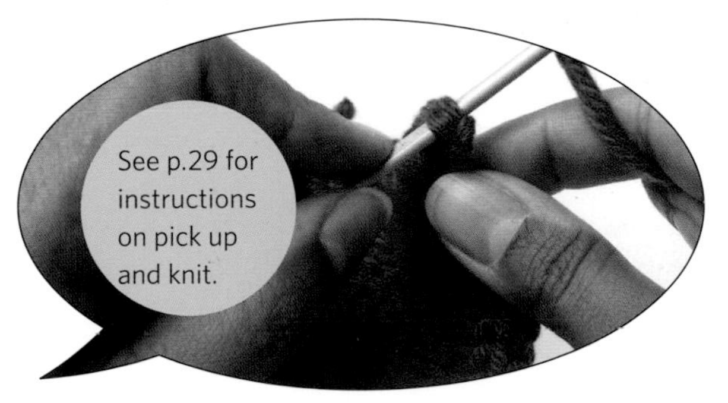

See p.29 for instructions on pick up and knit.

Count 21 (33, 38)sts on needle one – these are the stitches you just picked up plus the stitches you already had on that needle at the end of the heel-turning.

Needle two: Using a new needle (needle two), knit the 18 (30, 36) held non-heel sts – 9 (15, 18) from first needle and 9 (15, 18) from the next needle. All the stitches are now on two needles.

Needle three: Using a new needle (needle three), pick up and knit 9 (15, 18)sts (use the slipped sts as a guide).

Count 48 (78, 92)sts.

Knit 6 (9, 10)sts on to needle three from needle one.

Please note that the start of the round is now at the centre of the heel.

Count:

Needle 1: 15 (24, 28) sts.

Needle 2: 18 (30, 36) sts (front of sock).

Needle 3: 15 (24, 28) sts.

Total 48 (78, 92) sts.

Note to Knitters

Don't worry if it looks like there is a gap at the beginning and end of the pick-up-and-knit stitches – simply pull a little tighter the next time you knit a complete round and these will close up. If you find there is still a little hole, you can sew it up from the inside of the sock later on.

Now for the foot! You will notice that you are now working in the round again.

FOOT
ROUND 1
Needle one: K to last 3sts, K2tog, K1.
Needle two: K all sts.
Needle three: K1, SSK, K to end.
Count 46 (76, 90)sts.
ROUND 2
KNIT THE WHOLE ROUND
Repeat Rounds 1 and 2 until 36 (60, 72)sts remain, ending with a knit round.

Cross off numbers from the following chart to help you keep tally of this stage:

Babies/toddlers	Count				
Round 1	44	42	40	38	36
Round 2	K	K	K	K	K

Ladies	Count							
Round 1	74	72	70	68	66	64	62	60
Round 2	K	K	K	K	K	K	K	K

Men	Count								
Round 1	88	86	84	82	80	78	76	74	72
Round 2	K	K	K	K	K	K	K	K	K

Work in stocking stitch (knit every round) until the piece measures 9cm for the babies'/ toddlers' socks. For the ladies' and men's socks, you will need to measure the foot you are knitting for to get an exact fit. Measure from the end of the heel to the tip of the big toe and subtract 5cm. For example, a size 4 foot is 23cm from heel to toe, therefore you would work to 17cm. Be sure to end at the centre of the heel, as this marks the end of the round.

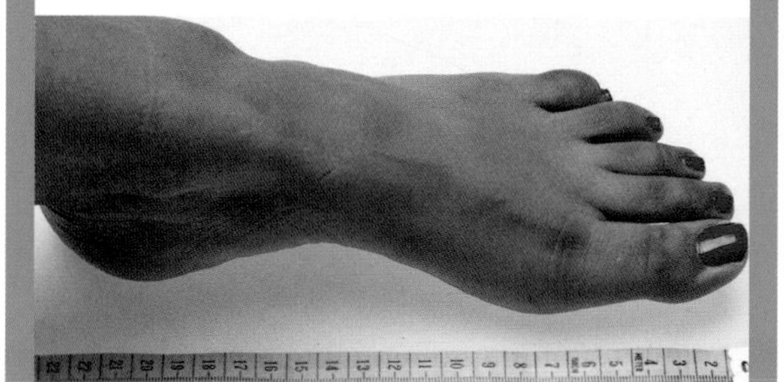

Measure from the tip of your big toe to the end of your heel - the entire length of the base of your foot, then subtract 5cm.

Once you have worked in stocking stitch until the foot of the sock reaches the appropriate length, decrease for the toe.

TOE

ROUND 1

Needle one: K to last 3sts, K2tog, K1.

Needle two: K1, SSK, K to last 3sts, K2tog, K1.

Needle three: K1, SSK, K to end.

Count 32 (56, 68)sts.

ROUND 2

Knit the whole round.

Repeat the last 2 rounds until 16 (28, 36)sts remain.

Use the following chart:

Babies/toddlers	Count			
Round 1	28	24	20	16
Round 2	K	K	K	K

Ladies	Count						
Round 1	52	48	44	40	36	32	28
Round 2	K	K	K	K	K	K	K

Men	Count							
Round 1	64	60	56	52	48	44	40	36
Round 2	K	K	K	K	K	K	K	K

Repeat Round 1 until 8 (8, 12)sts remain:

Babies/toddlers	12	8				
Ladies	24	20	16	12	8	
Men	32	28	24	20	16	12

Knit the stitches from needle one on to needle three - there will now be the same number of stitches on the two needles.

Cut the yarn, leaving a long tail for sewing up. Sew up the toe using Kitchener stitch (see p.26).

To finish, using the long tail of yarn you left when casting on, sew up the small opening at the top of the sock on the ribbed border. You don't have to worry too much about this; a few whip stitches (see p.36) will do the job nicely.

Weave in all ends.

Workshop: *Knitting straight on circular knitting needles*

Circular knitting needles come in different lengths as well as needle sizes. While the needle sizes are the same as for straight needles, it's the length that you'll need to think about in relation to your project, and the way you use your needles.

The length of a pair of circular needles includes the loose 'wire' section in between the needles.

Circular needles need not only be used for knitting in the round: they are a great way to work on a really wide piece of knitting that you wouldn't be able to fit on ordinary straight needles. As well as giving you more room for the stitches, the circular part of the needle will carry all the weight of the knitting, so that you don't have the strain of keeping the weight of a large piece of knitting on your wrists – as you would if you used straight needles.

When working straight on circular needles you simply use the circular needles as if they were straight needles. Push the stitches towards the tip of the needle on the end you are knitting on (the end with the working yarn) and push the stitches away from the needle at the end of your working row.

So, almost as if you are ignoring the circular wire of your needle, you can knit back and forth on the rows of your knitting.

This baby's blanket, knitted using 8 balls of the gorgeous Sublime Baby Cashmere Merino 4-ply Silk, was 310 stitches across. That number of stitches, combined with the weight of the knitting as it gets longer, means that it is much easier to use circular needles than straight ones.

PROJECT 10

Lengthways-striped scarf

YOU WILL NEED

DOUBLE KNIT YARN:
2 balls in colour A
and 2 balls in colour B

4.5MM CIRCULAR NEEDLE, 80/100CM LONG

START KNITTING

Cast on 250sts using colour A.

Knit 2 rows.

Join colour B without cutting colour A (see p.45 for two-colour stripes).

Knit 2 rows in colour B.

Pick up colour A again and continue in this way, knitting 2 rows in each colour, until your scarf is as wide as you want it to be (this one has about 60 rows in total).

Cast off and weave in the ends.

Handy HINT

You'll be hard pushed to follow Rule number two of knitting here (don't stop in the middle of a row), as each row is soooo long. What you need to remember, if you pick up your knitting in the middle of a row, is that the yarn should be on the right-hand side of the knitting. Pick up your knitting with the needles in each hand as if to start working: if the yarn you are knitting with is on the right-hand needle, you are good to go. If the yarn is on the left-hand needle, turn the work around in your hands so it's on the right-hand needle.

This scarf was knitted using Debbie Bliss Cashmerino DK. It has a cast-on of 250 stitches, so it makes sense to use circular needles. You need two balls of yarn in each colour, and as only about 2½ balls are used in the scarf, there should be sufficient yarn left over to make a matching stripey hat (use the pattern on p.98)! I suggest you use a knitting needle one size bigger than recommended for the yarn when knitting this scarf as your knitted fabric will have a slightly looser 'flow' and a more drapey effect when worn.

Workshop: ***Short row shaping***

This is a clever little technique for shaping your knitting so that there's more length on one side of the knitting than the other. It sounds a bit tricky, but don't worry, it will make sense when you get to it.

Short row shaping is often used on sock heels, or sometimes for subtle shaping on jumpers, cardigans and hats. My favourite way of using the technique is for a fun take on a simple scarf, as you'll see in a bit. Short row shaping is also known as 'wrap and turn' (W&T).

Here are the instructions for how to work short row shaping on a piece of garter stitch knitting. (It can be done on stocking stitch in the same way.)

ABBREVIATIONS

K = Knit

St(s) = Stitch(es)

K2tog = Knit two stitches together

W&T = Wrap and turn

YF = Yarn forward

Knitwise = Treat stitches as if you were about to knit them

Turn = Turning in the middle of a row means swapping the needles around in your hands, ready to start working in the other direction

How to wrap and turn

Knit according to your pattern instructions until you are asked to wrap and turn (W&T).

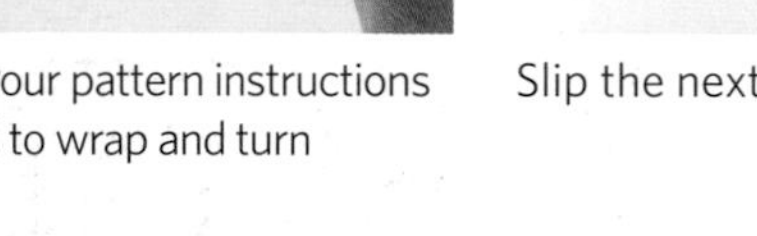

Slip the next stitch knitwise.

YF (bring the yarn to the front of the work).

Return the slipped stitch to the left-hand needle. This stitch now has the yarn wrapped around it – look closely at the base of the stitch.

Turn and work to the end. (If the next row is a purl row, bring the yarn forward

before purling to the end. If the next row is a knit row, leave the yarn at the back.)

Note to Knitters

Remember that if you are working the pattern in stocking stitch, at this point you would turn and purl to the end rather than knit.

You'll see that there is a little gap where you did the W&T.

Picking up the wrapped stitch

Knit until you get to one stitch before the gap – you'll see that is the stitch you have wrapped.

If you look very closely at the base of this stitch, you'll see the yarn you wrapped around it.

Pick up this wrap with the right-hand needle.

Then slip the wrapped stitch on to the right-hand needle knitwise. Now you have the wrap and wrapped stitch on the right-hand needle.

Insert the tip of the left-hand needle into the front of the top two stitches on the right-hand needle together.

You are now in the correct position to knit these two stitches together.

Continue knitting to the end of the row. You'll notice that the gap has been closed.

A pattern will probably tell you to work several rows with W&T in them, then pick up all the wraps in one row. As I say ... this will be a new technique to most of you and I don't want to you try and work it out until you have a pattern that uses short row shaping. It'll make sense when you get to it!

PROJECT 11

Table mat and coaster set

This pattern can be adapted to make coasters, table mats, or a twirly scarf. I know it sounds crazy to knit such unrelated projects from the same instructions, but I was designing the twirly scarf when I discovered the coaster! It works on any weight of yarn – with a thick yarn, the finished object will end up bigger than it would if knitted in a fine yarn. Experiment – it's the best way I know to discover new things and learn a lot!

Knitting isn't just for making garments and children's toys. You can make stylish additions to your home, too, such as this dinner set. This cool orange mat and coaster set is knitted using lovely self-patterning Artesano Hummingbird DK. I suggest that you knit a coaster before starting the mat.

YOU WILL NEED

(Makes 1 mat and 1 coaster)

134M DOUBLE KNIT YARN
(I used Artesano Hummingbird DK)

4MM KNITTING NEEDLES

GAUGE

This is not important for this sort of project, as it doesn't have to fit precisely.

ABBREVIATIONS

K = Knit

W&T = Wrap and turn (see workshop on short row shaping, p.122)

START KNITTING - COASTER

*Cast on 10sts.

Row 1: Knit 1 row.

Row 2: K8, W&T.

Row 3: Knit to end.

Row 4: K7, W&T.

Row 5: Knit to end.

Row 6: K6, W&T.

Row 7: Knit to end.

Row 8: K5, W&T.

Row 9: Knit to end.

Row 10: K4, W&T.

Row 11: Knit to end.

Row 12: K3, W&T.

Row 13: Knit to end.

Row 14: K2, W&T.

Row 15: Knit to end.

Row 16: K1, W&T.

Row 17: Knit to end

Here's what the knitting will look like after one repeat of Rows 1–17.

Row 18: Knit 1 row, picking up all wraps as you go (the wraps will be on all the stitches except for the first and last stitches).

Here's the knitting after a total of seven repeats of Rows 1–18. It is now ready to cast off.

Repeat last 18 rows a further six times (a total of seven times) to make a complete circle for the coaster*.

Cast off.

Sew up the coaster using whip stitch.

Making up the coaster. Leave a long tail of yarn, about 30cm, when you cast off. Use this tail and whip stitch (see p.36) to sew the coaster into a circle.

For a variation, knit the coaster using a textured yarn such as Stylecraft Eskimo DK, to end up with a fluffy snowflake pattern, which makes a great Christmas decoration.

START KNITTING – TABLE MAT

Cast on 30sts.

Row 1: Knit 1 row.

Row 2: K28, W&T.

Row 3: Knit to end.

Row 4: K27, W&T.

Row 5: Knit to end.

Row 6: K26, W&T.

Row 7: Knit to end.

Continue working in this way, knitting one fewer stitch before the wrap and turn on every even-numbered row.

When you have wrapped every stitch in the row apart from the first and last stitches, knit 1 row picking up all the wraps. As with the coaster, you'll have wraps on all the stitches except for the first and last stitches.

Starting from Row 1, repeat this sequence a further six times (seven in total) so you have a complete circle. Cast off and sew up the seam as for the coaster pattern.

PROJECT 12

Twirly scarf

A scarf doesn't always have to be a warm, woolly bundle of big knitting. I'm a firm believer that knitting can be used to make delicate, feminine, almost jewellery-like garments. This scarf can be knitted in anything from a fine, lace-weight yarn to a super-bulky yarn to create various effects.

YOU WILL NEED

4-PLY YARN

3.25MM KNITTING NEEDLES

This scarf has been knitted using half a ball of Araucania Ranco Solid, a beautiful sock yarn, and 3.25mm needles. (That works out to approximately 169m of any sock or 4-ply yarn.)

GAUGE

Not important for this project.

ABBREVIATIONS

K = Knit

W&T = Wrap and turn (see workshop on short row shaping, p.122)

START KNITTING

Follow pattern for the coaster from * to * (see p.124). Repeat until the scarf is as long as you want it to be.

Cast off.

Note to Knitters

The short row shaping shown on p.122 and the patterns for coasters, table mats and twirly scarf all use garter stitch. The technique is the same when knitting in stocking stitch; just remember that you need to knit and purl instead of knitting every row.

See the effect when you work from exactly the same pattern but using Rowan Big Wool and 10mm needles. It's worth experimenting with yarns and stitches to see what you can discover. That's how I came up with the patterns using short row shaping!

PROJECT 13

Create your own creature

I hate 'perfect' plastic dolls. As a child, my favourite teddy had no eyes! In this pattern, I've designed the basic outline of body and limbs and you have free rein to create an unlimited variety of creatures and characters.

Add personality as you create your creature.

You might find that your feline friends are fascinated by these little critters!

Hopefully these will be lots of fun to knit (as they were for me and my test knitters), so you can make a whole cast of quirky beings!

I've mostly used scraps of double knit yarn and 4mm needles, but this is a pattern where you can throw gauge-caution to the wind and use up any or all your oddments, in colour combinations of your choice. I'm a fan of colourful toys, but don't let that stop you knitting a more sober-suited character. For added charm, try putting a bell or two inside a little plastic container and sewing that into the body, wrapped in toy stuffing.

The only suggestion I might make regarding your yarn choice is washability. For children's toys, it's best to use a yarn that can be machine-washed to make life easier: I know my Mum probably had to wash my favourite toys by hand whilst I was asleep.

Go forth and create!

Note to Knitters

I hope that as well as embracing the creative side of this project, it will also help you to be braver technically. This really is an opportunity for you to design your own shapes, which is a step towards really understanding the structure of knitting and understanding the 'science bit' of your work.

YOU WILL NEED

YOU CAN USE ANY SCRAPS OF YARN FOR THE BODY
I'm using double knit yarn and 4mm needles, and by scraps, I mean less than a ball. Don't feel that you have to use the same brand for body and limbs – all normal rules for knitting go out of the window with this pattern!

STRAIGHT AND DOUBLE-POINTED KNITTING NEEDLES
in the appropriate size for your yarn

DARNING NEEDLE

TOY STUFFING

ODDMENTS AND IMAGINATION TO DECORATE

Handy HINT

See the yarn label for the needle size recommended by the manufacturer. If you knit with a loose tension, use a knitting needle one size smaller than recommended for the yarn. This will mean that the knitted fabric ends up with a tighter weave and the stuffing is less likely to show through.

ABBREVIATIONS

K = Knit

P = Purl

St(s) = Stitch(es)

St st = Stocking stitch

K2tog = Knit two stitches together

M1 = Make one stitch by picking up the loop in between two stitches

Cont = Continue

Rep = Repeat

START KNITTING

BODY

Cast on 6sts.

K 1 row.

P 1 row.

K1, [M1, K1] to end. Count 11sts.

P 1 row.

K1, [M1, K1] to end. Count 21sts.

P 1 row.

K1, [M1, K2] to end. Count 31sts.

Starting with a purl row, work in stocking stitch until piece measures approximately 8cm from beginning, ending with a purl row.

K1, [K2tog, K1] to end. Count 21sts.

P 1 row.

K2tog to last st, K1. Count 11sts.

P 1 row.

K 2tog to last st, K1. Count 6sts.

Finish with a drawstring finish.

Handy HINT

Here's an opportunity to give your character a shape of his or her own. If you work in stocking stitch for fewer than 8cm, the body will be a small, round shape. If you work for a few more centimetres, the character will be taller and skinnier. Also, you will need to knit more centimetres here if you are using thicker than double knit yarn. Another way of making the body bigger is to repeat the initial increase rows (probably best to do no more than a couple of these).

Note to Knitters

Remember that if you increase and add more stitches, you'll also need to work more decreases of [K2tog, K1] at the end of the pattern. But the main thing is not to worry and just experiment – the odder your character looks, the better, in my book. How amazing to have a knitting pattern where you simply can't go wrong!

Note to Knitters

If you've made the body bigger with more increases, simply work more decrease rows. The stitch count doesn't matter – just keep decreasing until you have 5-10sts before finishing.

Drawstring finish

Cut the yarn leaving a long tail, thread this onto a darning needle, run it through the remaining stitches, and pull tight.

Use the long tail of yarn on the darning needle to sew up the body along the seam using mattress stitch, but leave an opening of about 5cm.

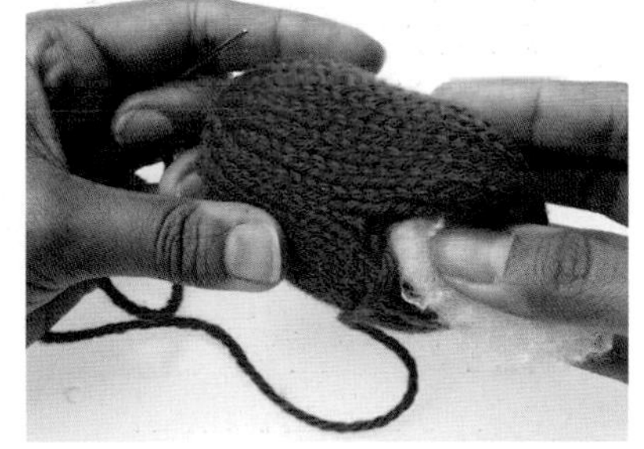

Stuff the body with toy stuffing and sew up completely, stuffing the last little bit as you go.

Weave in all the ends. You can hide the ends of the yarn by poking the darning needle with the yarn end right into the body and out the other side, pulling tightly, then snipping the yarn. Then squish the body about a bit, and the end will disappear into the belly!

Limbs

Using double-pointed needles and leaving a long tail of yarn for sewing the limb to the body, cast on 7sts and knit I-cord (see p.28) until the piece is as long or short as you like.

Finish with a drawstring finish or by casting off. Fasten off and weave in the end.

Note to Knitters

Please make sure that you sew on any embellishments really securely. Little people have a reputation for prising off buttons and stufing them up their noses, and we won't be having any of that here, please!

Make as many limbs and/or appendages as you need for the character and sew on securely.

You can add features using yarn, or by sewing on buttons or other embellishments.

PROJECT 14

Seasonal projects

Knitting isn't all about garments and keeping warm. You can use your knitting skills to knit little 'whimsies' to give as gifts or use as decorations. These also make great items to sell on stalls for your favourite charity.

Valentine's heart

Here's a fun way of using up oddments of yarn. As well as the whimsies shown below, you can sew the hearts onto clothing – they'd be so pretty on a hat or the Girls' pinafore dress (see p.66).

A little toy stuffing between two hearts makes a handy pincushion.

Here are two heart shapes sewn together, using a simple whip stitch, and then stuffed with dried lavender just before closing. With an added loop of yarn for hanging, this heart can add a soothing aroma to a bedside table, wardrobe, baby's cot or even your car.

YOU WILL NEED

ODDMENTS OF DOUBLE KNIT YARN
(I like a traditional red, but any colour will work)

3MM KNITTING NEEDLES
(I use a smaller needle than usual for DK yarn, as this makes the knitting stiffer so it can stand alone)

Handy HINT

If you'd like to use the heart as a Christmas tree decoration, you can block it for extra stiffness (see p.31).

Note to Knitters

I find it neater, on this pattern, to leave the tails of yarn a bit longer (about 20cm), so I can weave them in using a darning needle. This gives a tidier finish, as you won't have a seam to weave into. See p.44 for how to do a really neat finish.

GAUGE

Any double knit yarn and 3mm needles work with this pattern. Precise tension is not necessary.

ABBREVIATIONS

K = Knit
St(s) = Stitch(es)
K2tog = Knit two stitches together
M1 = Make one stitch
Rep = Repeat

START KNITTING

Cast on 3sts.

K 1 row.

K1, M1, K to end. (This is tricky when you've only worked 1 row, but persevere and it will become easier the more rows you knit.)

Repeat last row until you have 16sts.

Knit 10 rows.

K8sts, turn.

Rep last row a further four times (a total of 5 rows knitted on the first half of the top of the heart).

You will now be knitting the first side of the top of the heart to completion, leaving the other side on the needle and ignoring these 8sts for now.

K2tog, K to last 2sts, K2tog.

K2tog, K to last 2sts, K2tog.

Cast off.

You've now completed one side of the heart.

Rejoin the yarn to other side. See p.43 for how to rejoin yarn.

K8sts, turn.

Rep last row a further four times (a total of 5 rows knitted on the second half of the top of the heart).

K2tog, K to last 2sts, K2tog.

K2tog, K to last 2sts, K2tog.

Cast off.

Weave in all ends.

Easter bunny egg cosy

These egg cosies are fun and practical. Chocolate Easter eggs are one of the most over-packaged items you can buy. If a child received one from his parents, grandparents and an aunt or two, that's an awful lot of waste packaging.

Try giving instead a small chocolate egg wearing a fun and funky bunny cosy. The cosy can be used again and again, and you can also use it to cover boiled eggs for those without a sweet tooth.

The pattern is simple enough for knitters of all levels, with plenty of scope for customisation and personality.

YOU WILL NEED

- **SMALL AMOUNT OF DOUBLE KNIT YARN IN VARIOUS COLOURS**
- **4MM KNITTING NEEDLES**
- **DARNING NEEDLE**
- **ASSORTMENT OF BUTTONS AND COLOURED SEWING THREADS FOR EMBELLISHMENT**

GAUGE

Any double knit yarn and 4mm needles work with this pattern. A precise gauge is not necessary for this pattern.

START KNITTING

BODY

Cast on 24sts.

Knit every row until piece measures 5cm from beginning.

Now start decreasing for top of cosy:

[K1, K2tog] eight times. Count 16sts.

K 1 row.

[K1, K2tog] five times, K1. Count 11sts.

K 1 row.

[K1, K2tog] three times, K2. Count 8sts.

K 1 row.

Drawstring finish for top of egg cosy.

Cut the yarn, leaving a long tail. Thread this end onto a darning needle. Transfer the 8sts from the knitting needle to the darning needle one by one and pull tight.

Fold the egg cosy in half and sew up. See p.36 on sewing up garter stitch.

Weave in all ends.

EARS (MAKE TWO)

Cast on 5sts (leaving a long tail for sewing to the body).

Work in garter stitch until piece measures 3cm.

K2tog, K to end.

Repeat the last row until one stitch remains.

Fasten off.

Finishing

Pinch ears at the wide end and sew securely to the egg cosy – the pinch will add extra dimension to the ears.

Weave in all ends.

Turn your cosy into a bunny by sewing on features. I like buttons for eyes and an embroidered mouth, but use your imagination here, so that each bunny has an individual personality of its own.

Variations on the basic bunny can be made with different knitting stitches, colours and embellishments. Please note that the ears are always knitted as for the basic garter stitch bunny.

You could replace the garter stitch of the body with stocking stitch, add a ribbed border or use two-row colour stripes (see p.45). The characters don't always need ears – you could add yarn for hair and turn them into a mini-me of your favourite person. Here we have Raoul on the left and Mini-Pearson on the right. Let your imagination go wild, and don't forget to name your bunny!

Christmas tree

I love a bit of seasonal knitting. Here are some Christmas trees to get you into the holiday spirit. You can really go to town with your oddments, and it's a perfect excuse for using sparkly yarn and embellishments – not that I need an excuse. The more bling, the better!

Sew sparkly sequins and beads to a Christmas tree and use it as a tree ornament.

YOU WILL NEED

ODDMENTS OF DARK GREEN OR WHITE DOUBLE KNIT YARN

3MM KNITTING NEEDLES
(I use a smaller needle than usual for DK yarn, as this makes the knitted fabric stiffer, so it can stand alone)

SEQUINS, BEADS AND SEWING COTTON FOR EMBELLISHMENT

GAUGE

Any double knit yarn and 3mm needles work with this pattern. A precise gauge and knitting tension are not necessary.

ABBREVIATIONS

K = Knit

St(s) = Stitch(es)

K2tog = Knit two stitches together

START KNITTING

Cast on 16sts.

K 1 row.

K2tog, K to end.

Repeat last row until 8sts remain.

Knit 1 row.

Turn and cast on 4sts. Count 16sts.

Knit 1 row.

K2tog, K to end.

Repeat last row until 8sts remain.

Turn and cast on 4sts. Count 12sts.

Knit 1 row.

Turn and cast on 4sts. Count 16sts.

Knit 1 row.

K2tog, K to end.

Repeat until one stitch remains.

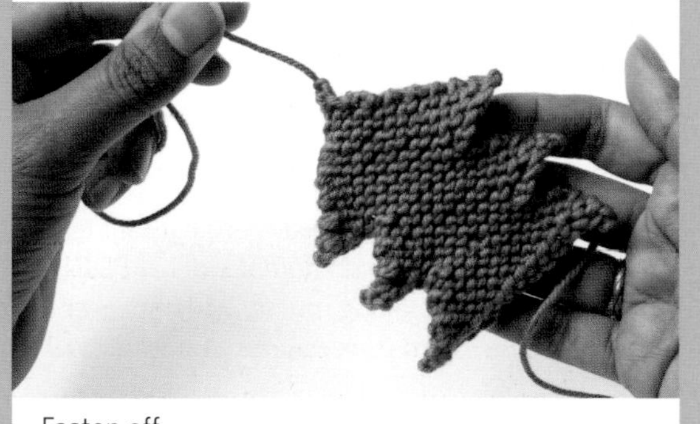

Fasten off.

Weave in all your ends.

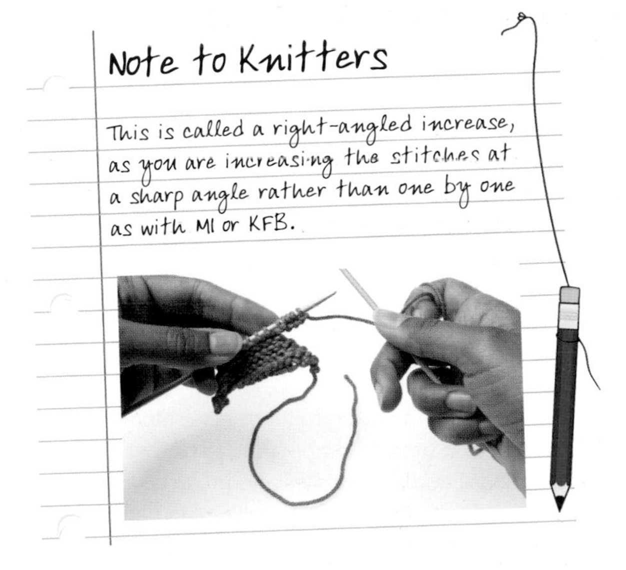

Finishing

Block the trees by spraying them with water on both sides, then sandwich between two tea towels, cover with heavy books and leave overnight. This will help your tree to hold its shape. See the difference here between the unblocked tree on the left and the blocked tree on the right.

Use beads and sequins to decorate your tree, and make a hanging loop from a piece of black cotton.

For instructions on how to turn your tree into a Christmas card, download the free PDF from www.knittingsos.co.uk.

Use the tree to make personalised Christmas cards for your loved ones. Putting the cards together might be a fun project to do with children.

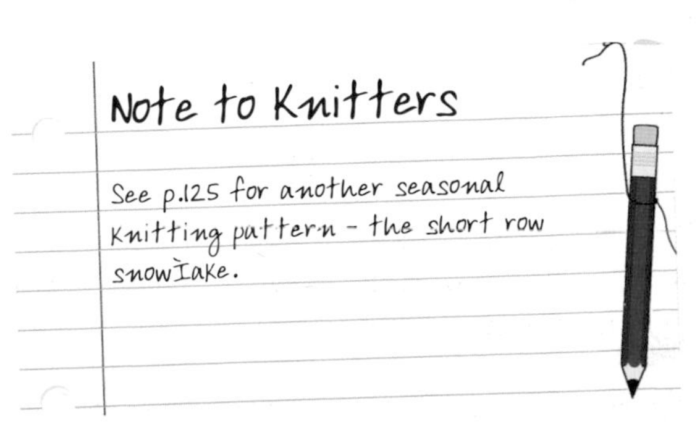

Stitch library

In this stitch library, you will learn some new ways to use knit and purl stitches, with some clever tricks thrown in to create all sorts of beautiful and fun textures in your knitting. Some of the techniques may seem very odd at first, but if you keep calm and concentrate, it won't be long before you are able to knit way beyond the basics of stocking stitch and rib. You'll learn just how many exciting effects you can get with the craft of knitting!

Do (kn)it yourself

This stitch library can be used to learn new stitches, or for taking your first steps in simple pattern design. I'll give you the basic tools of stitches and projects, and show you how to work out your own knitting patterns for the project of your choice in the stitch and yarn of your choice. Get ready to start designing! If you follow the steps on the right, you can learn how to knit something completely unique. All it takes is a bit of vision and some 'knitting-maths'.

In the next few pages, as well as learning the stitches and how to use them in your designs, you'll see some of the projects created by my team of amazing test knitters – who are all advanced-beginner or intermediate knitters, just like you!

Step 1: *Choose a project.*

Step 2: *Choose a stitch pattern.*

Step 3: *Knit a practice square – VERY IMPORTANT!*

Step 4: *Decide on the width of knitting you need for the pattern.*

Step 5: *Do the maths to get the correct number of stitches to start with.*

Step 6: *Start knitting!*

Step 7: *Some projects will need specific finishing techniques (you can download free PDFs on how to finish a bag, purse, cushion cover or greetings card from www.knittingsos.co.uk)*

Step 1: The projects

Here are a number of projects that you can design yourself. First, choose what you'd like to knit:

- **Bag**
- **Purse**
- **Baby blanket**
- **Shawl/wrap/scarf**
- **Cushion cover**
- **Greetings cards**
- **Afghan**
- **Or choose something else you'd like to make. Stick to simple shapes for now, as this is your first time designing your own knitting pattern.**

Example project: I've decided I want to knit a cushion cover.

Step 2: The stitches

Now choose which stitch you'd like to use to knit your project in:

Wrap drop stitch (p.142)

Fireside lace stitch (p.144)

Cable plait stitch (p.146)

Six-toed cable stitch (p.147)

Cable twist stitch (p.148)

Bramble stitch (p.150)

Bobble stitch (p.151)

Loopy stitch (p.154)

Knitting with beads (p.156)

Fir tree lace stitch (p.158)

Knit and purl motifs (p.162)

Moss zig stitch (p.163)

Fair Isle or intarsia (p.164)

Swiss darning (p.170)

Example project: I'd like to have a go at designing my own Fair Isle chart for my cushion cover.

Step 3: Knit a practice square

Knit a practice square in the stitch of your choice, using the exact yarn and needles you want to use for the finished project. This step is essential for figuring out the maths of the final project and to get you used to a new stitch.

Example project: I'm going to use Cascade 220, which knits up on 4.5mm knitting needles.

Example project: Here's my test square – it took a few pieces of knitter's graph paper before I got the pattern I wanted. It was tricky getting a pattern that would repeat correctly!

Example project: I measured my test square to be approximately 11cm wide.

Step 4: Decide on the width of your knitting

Example project: My cushion pad is about 40cm square, so I want my cushion cover to be about 35 cm square.

Step 5: Do the knitting maths

Multiply the size of your practice square to the width you want for your finished project. You need to multiply the number of stitches you cast on in your practice square to get to the nearest approximate centimetre to your chosen final width.

Example project: If I want my final cushion cover to be about 35cm wide, that means I need to cast on approximately three times the number of stitches in my test square, and repeat my chart three times.

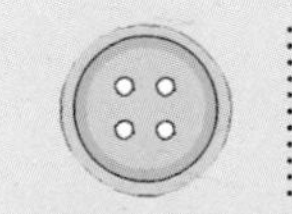

Handy HINT

Once you've sorted out the measurements and numbers, stop for a cup of tea! Designing knitting patterns takes a lot of maths and if you are anything like me, most of your mathematical knowledge was forgotten the day after you finished your last maths test at school. Now you have completed steps 1–5, you're nearly at the fun bit!

Handy HINT

Designing your own pattern will mean a certain amount of trial and error. When I'm designing something, I know I'll have to undo and re-knit it at least three times before getting it right! This is just part of the process of creating something completely new. There are millions of knitting patterns out there if you decide designing isn't for you, but if you give it a go I promise you will find it satisfying in the end!

Step 6: Start knitting!

You've got some lovely yarn and chosen a stitch pattern. Now there's nothing but a bit of knitting between you and a unique, personally designed piece of knitting.

If you are repeating a pattern from the stitch library, you can use markers (or contrasting bits of yarn, as shown here) to show you when to start each repeat of the pattern. This will be especially useful if you are knitting a wide piece of knitting with many repeats, such as a baby blanket.

Example project

Step 1: *I've chosen to knit a cushion cover.*

Step 2: *I'd like to use Fair Isle and design my own pattern.*

Step 3: *First of all I knit a practice square in stocking stitch with the Fair Isle design I've plotted onto a chart of knitters' graph paper (see p.161). My practice square was 24sts wide, which measured 11cm.*

Step 4: *I wanted to make a cushion cover about 35cm wide.*

Step 5: *So the maths told me to make my cast on three times the number of stitches of my practice square. That gets me to 72sts = 33cm (it's best to knit your cushion cover a bit smaller than the cushion pad so it stretches tight over the pad to best effect).*

Step 6: *I cast on 72sts and started knitting in my chosen pattern until it became square. Then I cast off and knit the back pieces of the cushion.*

Step 7: *Download a free PDF at www.knittingsos.co.uk for instructions on sewing up and finishing a cushion cover.*

Handy **HINT**

When knitting a new stitch, it's worth keeping a tally as you knit the rows so you always know where you are in the pattern. It's important to follow the stitch patterns accurately!

Note to Knitters

This maths is an approximate process, in that you may not get the width you planned to the exact centimetre, but only to the nearest centimetre or two. This approximation is Ïne for all the projects here, as they do not have to be knitted to an exact measurement.

The stitches

Wrap drop stitch

This is a great stitch to learn if you are new to stitch patterns. If you can cast on, cast off and do a basic knit stitch, then you can handle wrap drop. You don't even need to purl!

Wrap drop stitch

Cast on any number of stitches.

Knit 5 rows.

Wrap row: Wrap every stitch three times.

Drop row: Knit every stitch, dropping the wraps as you go.

Knit 5 rows.

Repeat last 7 rows until piece is as long as you want it to be.

Cast off.

Try knitting this stitch using a ribbon yarn for a very different effect from that of a traditional wool yarn. A couple of skeins of Colinette Giotto is a good ribbon yarn to try.

Knitting can be glamorous! This scarf has been knitted using Rowan Shimmer in a sparkly black. You only need 1 or 2 balls, as it goes a long way. I think that the extra-long tassels really add to the finish of this piece.

How to work wrap drop stitch

Cast on any number of stitches – 20 is a good number for a practice square. Knit 5 rows to begin with.

ROW 1 (WRAP ROW):

Pick up a stitch.

Wrap the yarn around the right-hand needle three times (back and middle three times). Use your left index finger to hold the wraps on the needle.

Complete the stitch. You'll now have 3 stitches on the right-hand needle.

Continue in the same way for the rest of the row, wrapping each stitch three times. You'll end up with three times the number of stitches you started with.

ROW 2 (DROP ROW):

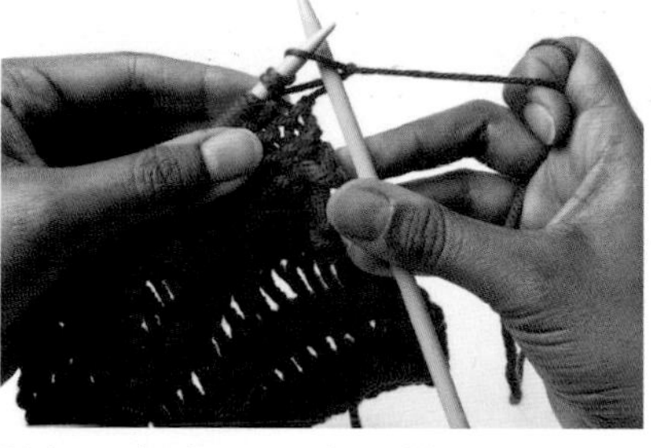

Pick up the first stitch and knit it.

When you release the stitch, the extra wraps will automatically be released too. Don't worry about dropping

stitches, as only the wraps will release themselves.

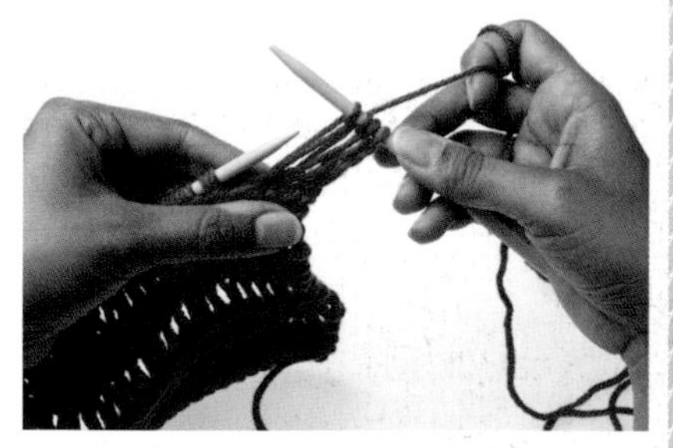

Continue knitting to the end of the row, dropping the wraps as you go.

When you get to the end of the drop row, you'll see the effect of the wrap drop stitch and you'll be able to count the same number of stitches that you cast on initially. Give your knitting a little tug to even out the wrap drops.

Next knit 5 rows – this creates a garter stitch band in between the wraps to show them off to their best advantage.

Fireside lace stitch

This stitch is a simple way to start your lace-knitting career. It uses a simple repeat of YF (yarn forward) to create a very clever-looking piece of knitting and a pretty lace stitch. It can be translated into a scarf or a shawl, or if you're feeling particularly creative, why not give it a contrasting lining and make it into a cushion cover?

This glamorous evening bag has been knitted up and then inserted into a purse frame (see free PDF on www.knittingsos.co.uk for how to do this). It was lined in a contrasting colour that shows through the lace stitches.

This light summer wrap uses 5 balls of Sublime Bamboo and Pearls DK and 4mm needles. To knit it, cast on 66sts and knit fireside lace to approximately 130cm.

Fireside lace stitch

ABBREVIATIONS

YF = Yarn forward

YF2 = Yarn forward twice

YF3 = Yarn forward three times

YF4 = Yarn forward four times

Cast on a multiple of 10sts plus 6sts (for example 26sts, as I have done below).

Row 1: Knit 1 row.

Row 2: Knit 1 row.

Row 3: K6, [YF2, K1, YF3, K1, YF4, K1, YF3, K1, YF2, K6], rep to end.

Row 4: Knit the row, dropping all the extra wraps. Count to ensure you have the same number of stitches you started with.

Row 5: Knit 1 row.

Row 6: Knit 1 row.

Row 7: K1, [YF2, K1, YF3, K1, YF4, K1, YF3, K1, YF2, K6], rep to end. On the last repeat, you will end with a K1 instead of a K6.

Row 8: As Row 4.

Repeat last 8 rows until piece is as long as you want it to be, ending with a Row 2.

Cast off.

How to knit multiple yarn forwards

YF (yarn forward) is when you bring the yarn to the front of your work, as if you were about to purl (although your next stitch won't necessarily be a purl stitch).

YF2 = Bring the yarn to the front of the work, then bring it forwards again by wrapping it around the right-hand needle anti-clockwise.

YF3 = Bring the yarn to the front, then again another two times by wrapping it around the right-hand needle twice anti-clockwise. You have now brought the yarn forward a total of three times.

YF4 = Bring the yarn to the front, then again another three times by wrapping it around the right-hand needle three times anti-clockwise. You have now brought the yarn forward a total of four times.

After knitting a wrap row, you'll notice that you have lots of extra stitches bunched up on the needle - don't panic, as these will disappear after the next row.

How to drop extra wraps

When you knit the row where you drop the extra wraps, knit until you get to the wraps, and then simply push them off the left-hand needle. You'll see that they aren't proper stitches, but are just wrapped around the left needle without being attached to the work. Don't worry about dropping anything you shouldn't, as the next proper stitch to be knitted will be firmly on the needle, unlike the wraps. Don't worry if all this seems a bit daunting; remember that you'll have done all your practice on a test square before you put this stitch into a garment, so you'll be an expert by the time you start your main project.

You'll spot the proper stitch, as distinct from the wraps, by its little 'collar'. This is a small, horizontal bit of yarn at the base of the stitch, which is holding it firmly on the needle. The wraps don't have this 'collar', so they will just fall off the needle as you are knitting Rows 4 and 8.

At the end of the drop row you'll have the same number of stitches that you started with.

Note to Knitters

After working the drop row, you'll notice that the stitches and lace sections look uneven. You can ﬁx this by gently pulling the work after each drop row. Hold the needle in one hand and pull the knitting down and away from it with the other.

Workshop: *How to cable*

A cable is a pattern that looks like a twisted section against a background of garter or stocking stitch. Once you learn how to create a basic twist, you can experiment and knit all sorts of beautiful patterns.

To do cable knitting, you need a cable needle. This is a small knitting needle with a V-shaped or U-shaped bend in it. Stitches are transferred on to this so that they can be knitted in a different order.

You slip the stitches on to the cable needle without knitting them, so they can be held out of the way whilst you knit the next stitches.

The two basic techniques are cable forwards (CF) and cable back (CB). The actual cable pattern itself will vary, depending on the knitting pattern, and will be written out at the beginning of the pattern; but as long as you know how to CF and CB you'll be able to follow any cable instruction.

CF (cable forward). This is when you place some stitches on a cable needle and hold them to the front of your work.

CB (cable back). This is when you place some stitches on a cable needle and hold them to the back of your work.

Cable plait stitch

Here's one of my favourite cable patterns: cable plait. It's a good starter cable pattern as you get to use CF (cable forwards) and CB (cable back), and you end up with an impressive pattern!

Note to Knitters

Both the cable patterns shown here are on a garter stitch background, so you can use them to knit scarves that won't curl up (as they would if they were on a traditional reverse stocking stitch background – this is when the purl is the right side and the knit is the wrong side of the work).

Cable plait stitch

ABBREVIATIONS

CF6 = slip 3sts on to cable needle and hold to the front of the work, knit the next 3sts, slip the 3sts from the cable needle back to the left-hand needle, knit these 3sts

CB6 = slip 3sts on to cable needle and hold to the back of the work, knit the next 3sts, slip the 3sts from the cable needle back to the left-hand needle, knit these 3sts

Cast on a multiple of 21sts (for example 21sts as I've shown here, or 42sts if you want the cable pattern repeated twice, etc.).

Row 1 (RS): K 1 row.

Row 2 (WS): K6, P9, K6 (if you are making the pattern more than one multiple, you would repeat all these instructions again from the beginning, to the end of the row).

Row 3 (RS): K6, CB6, K9. Repeat from beginning to end.

Row 4 (WS): As Row 2.

Row 5 (RS): K 1 row.

Row 6 (WS): As Row 2.

Row 7 (RS): K9, CF6, K6. Repeat from beginning to end.

Row 8 (WS): K6, P9, K6. Repeat from beginning to end.

Repeat last 8 rows until piece is as long as you want it to be, ending with a RS row.

Cast off on the WS of your work in pattern.

This pretty scarf is knitted using two repeats of the cable plait pattern with a cast-on of 42sts, and 2 balls of Sirdar Click DK.

Aneeta's six-toed cable stitch

Designing your own cable stitch isn't something I recommend, but I couldn't resist having a go, and after lots of maths, undoing and re-knitting, here it is. I'm calling it Aneeta's six-toed cable stitch and no, I don't have six toes – I just thought it would be a funny name as the cable has six strands to the pattern. It's a more complicated-looking cable design, which I think is pretty and very satisfying to knit. As I've put it on a garter stitch background and not a reverse stocking stitch, as is traditional for cable patterns, this stitch won't curl and would make a great scarf.

This bag was knitted with 1½ balls of Debbie Bliss Cashmerino DK and two repeats of the stitch pattern (that's a cast-on of 48sts). Download a free PDF from www.knittingsos.co.uk for instructions on how to sew on bag handles.

This stitch takes a bit of extra concentration, so I suggest you work a practice square before you start.

Aneeta's six-toed cable stitch

ABBREVIATIONS

CF4 = slip 2sts on to cable needle and hold to the front of the work, knit the next 2sts, slip the 2sts from the cable needle back to the left needle, knit these 2sts

CB4 = slip 2sts on to cable needle and hold to the back of the work, knit the next 2sts, slip the 2sts from the cable needle back to the left-hand needle, knit these 2st

Cast on a multiple of 24sts (for example 24sts, as I've shown here, or 48sts if you want the cable pattern repeated twice, etc.).

Row 1 (RS): K 1 row.

Row 2 (WS): K6, P12, K6. Repeat from beginning to end

Row 3 (RS): K6, CF4, CF4, CF4, K6. Rep from beginning to end of the row, depending on how many repeats of the pattern you're knitting.

Row 4 (WS): As Row 2.

Row 5 (RS): K 1 row.

Row 6 (WS): As Row 2.

Row 7 (RS): K8, CB4, CB4, K8. Rep from beginning to end.

Row 8 (WS): As Row 2.

Repeat last 8 rows until piece is as long as you want it to be, ending with a RS row.

Cast off on the WS of your work in pattern.

Knit a cosy snood from approximately 1½ balls of Rowan Big Wool and 12 mm knitting needles. Cast on 24sts and repeat the pattern for 60 cm, then cast off. Sew into a tube.

Cable twist stitch

This stitch gives the impression of a very fine cable, but it's knitted without using a cable needle. I have to say that this is one of my favourite stitches to knit, as it's a really simple process to get such a pretty result. I'm planning to knit a delicate baby's blanket using cable twists.

Note to Knitters

As this stitch is based on a 2 x 2 rib pattern, you can use it for any project that has a 2 x 2 ribbed border - it would make a pretty addition to socks.

Cable twist

ABBREVIATIONS

CT = Cable twist

Cast on a multiple of 4sts plus 2sts (for example 22sts, as I have done below).

Row 1 (RS): K2, [P2, CT], rep to last 4sts, P2, K2.

Row 2 (WS): P2, K2, rib to end – you will start and end this row with P2.

Row 3 (RS): K2, P2, rib to end – you will start and end this row with K2.

Row 4 (WS): P2, K2, rib to end – you will start and end this row with P2.

Repeat last 4 rows until piece is as long as you want it to be.

Cast off in pattern.

This scarf has been knitted using an amazing hand-dyed yarn from Prick Your Finger. You can really experiment with your yarn choices when using the Stitch library.

How to knit cable twist

Knit 2sts together, but DON'T release the two stitches from the left-hand needle.

Insert the right-hand needle into the top stitch on the left-hand needle (one of the two you just knitted together).

Knit that stitch.

Then release both of the two original stitches that you knitted together.

Bramble stitch

Bramble stitch is surprisingly quick to knit once you get the hang of it, and really shows the limitless options for what you can create once you can knit and purl.

See the free PDF at www.knittingsos.co.uk for how to finish a purse using a frame.

Bramble stitch

ABBREVIATIONS

MB = Make bramble

P3tog = Purl 3sts together

Cast on a multiple of 4sts plus 2sts (for example 22sts).

Row 1 (RS): P 1 row.

Row 2 (WS): K1, [MB, P3tog], rep to last st, K1.

Row 3 (RS): P 1 row.

Row 4 (WS): K1, [P3tog, MB], rep to last st, K1.

Repeat last 4 rows until piece is as long as you want it to be.

Cast off.

This pretty scarf is knitted in 4-ply Araucania Ranco Solid. You only need half a ball for a cute kiddy scarf.

How to make a bramble

Pick up the stitch and knit it, but DON'T release the stitch from the left-hand needle.

Bring the yarn to the front of the work.

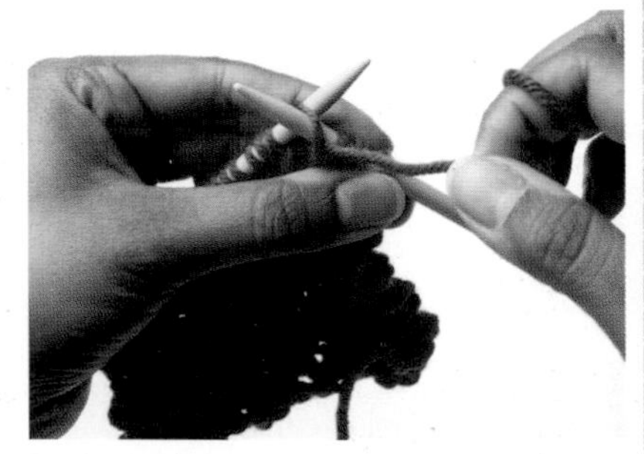

Purl into the same stitch again, and again DON'T release the stitch from the left-hand needle.

Take the yarn to the back of the work and knit into the same stitch again.

Now that you have knit, purl, knit into the same stitch, you can release that stitch from the left-hand needle.

Then purl the next 3sts together. This means that you will have the same number of stitches at the end of the row that you had at the beginning of the row. Remember to count them!

Bobble stitch

Knitting bobbles into your knitting can turn a simple project into something instantly zany. Whilst I'm not sure I'll be knitting all my jumpers with bobbles on them, I definitely think they work as a fun twist on a simple scarf, or as a border to a pair of gloves. You can add a bobble anywhere you wish in your knitting, on any number of stitches or any stitch background – use your imagination!

Cast on 29sts using Debbie Bliss Cashmerino DK for this cool 'dragon-skin' bobble scarf.

Bobble stitch

ABBREVIATION

MB = Make bobble

I've knitted my test square on a garter stitch background. This means the knitting won't curl up and would work nicely as a scarf.

Cast on a multiple of 7sts + one stitch (for example 22sts, as I have done here).

Row 1 (WS): K1, [K3, MB, K3], repeat to end.

Rows 2, 3, 4, 5, 6: Knit these rows.

Row 7 (WS): MB, [K6, MB], repeat to end.

Rows 8, 9, 10, 11, 12: Knit these rows.

Repeat last 12 rows until piece is as long as you want it to be, ending with a Row 8.

Cast off.

How to make bobble stitch

To make a bobble, you have to knit into the same stitch five times. You do this on the WS of the work, so the bobble appears on the other side.

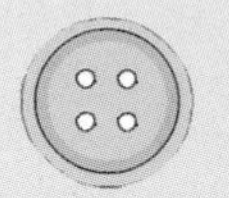

Handy **HINT**

Remember that you can make the bobbles as close together or as far apart as you like. You can even take the challenge of making a chart and adding bobbles to create a letter, name or motif. This would work really well on a garter stitch scarf.

First, knit into the front of the stitch as if it were a regular knit stitch – but DON'T release the stitch from the left-hand needle.

Then, knit into the back of the same stitch (see section knitting into the front and back of a stitch, p.23) and DON'T release the stitch from the left-hand needle.

Then knit into the front of the stitch again without releasing the stitch from the left-hand needle.

And then knit into the back of the same stitch again (this is the fourth time you've knitted into the original stitch).

Finally, knit into the front of the stitch (this is the fifth time you've knitted into the same stitch).

This time, release the stitch from the left-hand needle.

This is how your knitting will look when you've knitted into the front, back, front, back, and front of the same stitch.

Turn the work and knit those 5sts.

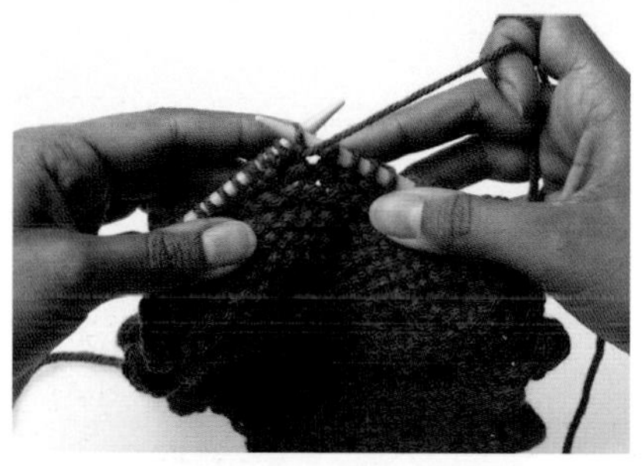
Turn the work and purl those 5sts.

Then turn and knit the 5sts and finally turn and purl the 5sts.

To complete the bobble, with the WS of the work facing you, take the yarn to the back and then one by one, lift the 4 extra stitches you knitted over the stitch at the top of the right-hand needle – as if you were casting them off one at a time.

You'll see that once you've lifted all 4sts over the top stitch on the right-hand needle, you are left only with only one stitch instead of the 5sts you started with.

Handy **HINT**

Poke your finger into the back of the bobble at this stage to make sure it's facing the right way – this is, away from you and towards the RS of the knitting.

Then simply continue working until you are ready to make another bobble.

Questions & Answers

Is there a way of knitting this stitch so that the bobbles appear on both sides of the knitting?

Yes! Instead of knitting 5 plain knit rows in between the bobble rows, knit 4 rows (or any even number). That way, the bobbles will alternate from one side of the work to the other.

Loopy stitch

OK ... I know it's a bit mad and 70s, but I couldn't resist showing you how to do loopy stitch. I don't really think it would work on an entire cardigan or jumper (but please feel free to try this out if you dare: my sister and I had matching pink loopy cardigans back in the day!) – how about using it for the border of a scarf, gloves or jumper? First person brave enough to knit a bathmat wins a prize!

Loopy stitch

ABBREVIATIONS

ML = Make loop

YF = Yarn forward

Cast on any number of stitches (for example 12sts, as I have done here).

Row 1 (WS): Knit 1 row.

Row 2 (RS): ML, repeat to end, making a loop in every stitch.

Repeat last 2 rows until piece is as long as you want it to be.

Cast off on the wrong side.

These glamorous gloves have been knitted with a loopy stitch border instead of rib (see p.90 for glove pattern) and require 154m double knit yarn (the pretty pair pictured used about half a skein of self-patterning Manos del Uruguay Silk Blend). They are so luxurious!

How to make a loop

Knit the stitch but DO NOT release it from the left-hand needle.

Bring the yarn to the front of the work in between the needles (YF).

Wrap the yarn clockwise around your thumb (as you look at it from the top) and take it to the back of the work in between the needles.

Now knit into the same stitch again and release it from the left-hand needle. You'll be left with 2 stitches on the right-hand needle.

Lift the first (lower) stitch over the second stitch (as if you were casting it off). This holds the loop securely in place.

Repeat this process for every stitch. When you get to the end of the row, I suggest you give a quick tug to every loop to straighten them out.

I know this stitch feels a bit odd to knit, but persevere – I think it's a fun one to impress your knitting or even non-knitting friends.

Knitting with beads

Knitting beads in with your yarn really adds an extra dimension to your fabric and can be used to great decorative effect on any of your classic projects.

Here's a handy glasses case. See the free PDFs at www.knittingsos.co.uk for how to finish your knitting with a purse frame.

Knit with beads

ABBREVIATIONS

YF = Yarn forward

YB = Yarn back

PB = Place bead

SL1P = Slip one stitch purlwise

To knit the square below, I threaded 36 beads on to the yarn. You can use any yarn. Choose beads with a hole that is the right size to allow them to slide on to the yarn easily.

For this square I started by casting on 20sts.

Starting with a knit row, work in stocking stitch for 6 rows, ending with a purl row.

Row 1 (RS): K3, YF, PB, SL1P, YB, [K5, YF, PB, SL1P, YB], rep to last 4sts, K4.

Row 2 (WS): P 1 row.

Row 3 (RS): K4, YF, PB, SL1P, YB, [K5, YF, PB, SL1P, YB], rep to last 3sts, K3.

Row 4 (WS): P 1 row.

Row 5 (RS): K5, YF, PB, SL1P, YB, [K5, YF, PB, SL1P, YB], rep to last 2sts, K2.

Row 6 (WS): P 1 row.

Row 7 (RS): K6, YF, PB, SL1P, YB, [K5, YF, PB, SL1P, YB], rep to last st, K1.

Row 8 (WS): P 1 row.

Repeat last 8 rows until piece is as long as you want it to be.

Cast off.

How to place a bead in your knitting

Before you start knitting, you must thread all the beads you need on to the yarn. This can be a tricky process – try using something called a big eye needle, which you can find in bead shops. Also be sure to use a bead that slides on to the yarn easily.

Using this method, you can place beads wherever you wish on your knitting. They can make a pattern, be randomly scattered, or even carefully placed to form a letter or a shape.

Knit until you are ready to add a bead.

Bring the yarn to the front of your work (YF).

Slide the bead down so it rests on the knitting (PB).

Slip the next stitch as if you were purling (SL1P).

Take the yarn to the back of the work (YB), making sure you hold the bead to the front.

Continue knitting, making sure that you knit the first stitch after the bead firmly.

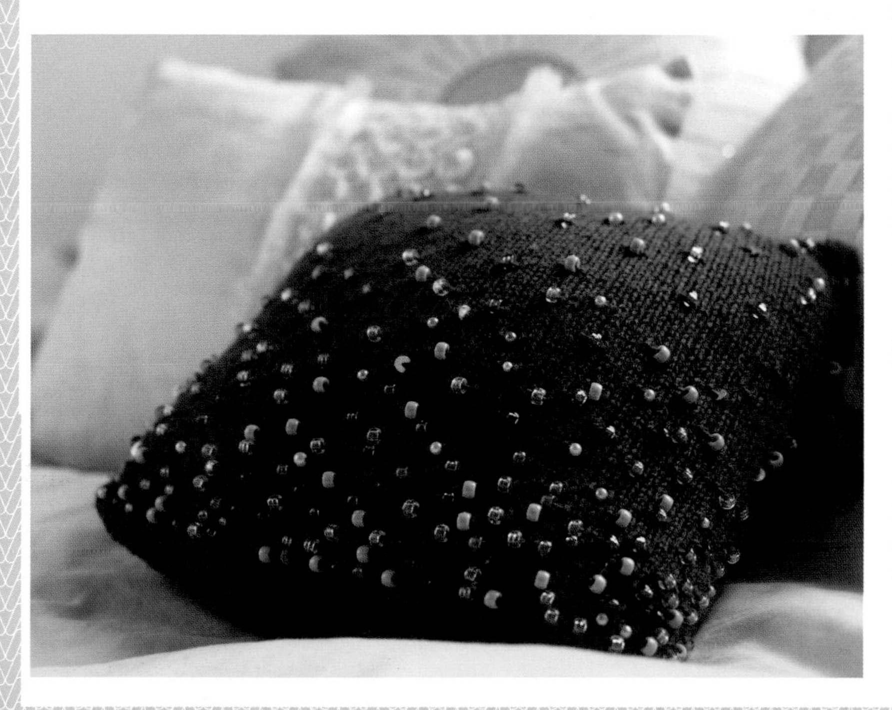

Handy **HINT**

If the bead shows on the wrong side of the work, you may not be knitting the first stitch after the bead firmly enough. You can remedy this by simply poking the bead through to the right side of the knitting, where it should stay neatly in place.

You can scatter a mixture of beads (and sequins) anywhere you fancy as you are knitting. Just remember that all embellishments have to be threaded on to the yarn first.

See www.knittingsos.co.uk for how to make and finish a cushion cover.

Fir tree lace stitch

This lace pattern is a little more advanced. It will take some dedication, but the end result is very satisfying. I know that some of you will look at this pattern and think, "Argh! Run for the hills!" But don't panic ... Just take each stitch and each row at a time, work slowly, mark off the rows as you work them and remember the Four Rules of Knitting. You'll be fine!

Handy HINT

Lace is best knitted with a great deal of care and patience. If you are feeling tired, pick up some simpler knitting and save the lace for when you have more energy. There's no point in struggling with it. And it's definitely not a project to be knitting after a glass or two of wine!

Fir tree lace

ABBREVIATIONS

YO = Wrap the yarn around the right-hand needle anti-clockwise

P2SSO = Pass two slipped stitches over

SK2 = Slip a stitch knitwise, then slip the next stitch knitwise

SSK = Slip, slip, knit (see p.22)

Cast on a multiple of 10sts plus one stitch (for example 21sts, as I have done below).

Row 1 (WS): P 1 row.

Row 2 (RS): K1, *[YO, SSK] twice, K1, [K2tog, YO] twice, K1. Rep from *. Count to ensure you've got the same number of stitches you started with - they'll look twisted, so take care to count accurately.

Row 3 (WS): P 1 row.

Row 4 (RS): K2, *[YO, SSK, YO, SK2, K1, P2SSO, YO, K2tog, YO, K3]. Rep from * (on the last repeat you'll end with K2 instead of K3). Count to ensure you've got the same number of stitches you started with.

Repeat last 4 rows until piece is as long as you want it to be.

Cast off.

This beautiful shawl, with a cast-on of 201sts, was made with 2½ skeins of Manos del Uruguay Fairtrade lace yarn - and it nearly doubled in size after blocking (see p.31). It was pinned out to measure 50 x 125cm, then steam-blocked. The first time that you block lace, the difference in size and texture will amaze you!

How to work fir tree lace stitch

YO: wrap the yarn around the right-hand needle anti-clockwise.

P2SSO: pass 2 slipped stitches over.

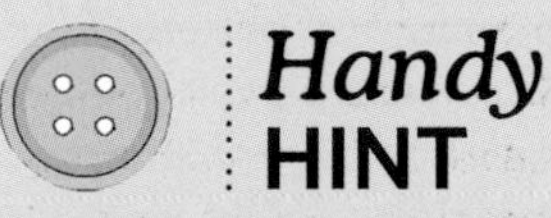

Handy HINT

Don't forget to mark off each row as you've done it. It will be hard to keep track of where you are otherwise.

Note to Knitters

After working a lace row, the stitches will look a bit wonky. Take care to knit these carefully. Sometimes the stitches will look crossed over - this is where you did a YO. Sometimes the stitches will look as if they are twisted. In this case, roll them towards you as the stitches on the top are the correct ones.

Handy HINT

See p.41 for how to do a saver row. I found this was invaluable when I insisted on watching telly at the same time as knitting fir tree lace. When I made a mistake through a lapse of concentration, it saved me from having to undo the knitting all the way back to the beginning.

This scarf, knitted with 2 balls of Debbie Bliss Cashmerino DK, hasn't been blocked, so you can see the curled-up effect of this stitch.

How to follow a chart

Stitch and colourwork patterns (any means of incorporating colour, such as with stripes, Fair Isle or intarsia) are often shown on a chart, as well as being written out. Following a chart can seem daunting, but it's really very simple if you follow a few basic rules:

1. **Read a chart from the bottom up.**
2. **Read knit rows from right to left.**
3. **Read purl rows from left to right.**
4. **Tick off rows as you do them, so you always know where you are.**
5. **Remember to count your stitches carefully, so you follow the pattern accurately.**

The chart for the heart motif below has 21sts and 29 rows. The pattern starts on stitch 11 of Row 7 – this is a knit row, so you read it from right to left.

If you were working this pattern in colourwork, you would use intarsia, with three separate bobbins of yarn: one for the heart and two for the background to the left and right of the heart. When you get to the top of the heart where there's a patch of background between the two 'bumps' of the heart; here you would add a third bobbin for the background. (For instructions on intarsia, see p.167.)

If you were working this pattern in Swiss darning (see p.170), you would start by knitting the background square, casting on 21sts and working in stocking stitch for 29 rows. The heart motif would then be sewn on top.

Start reading a chart from the bottom and work your way up. (Please note that the grey squares are just for information.)

K																						29
P																						28
K																						27
P																						26
K																						25
P							X	X						X	X							24
K						X	X	X	X				X	X	X	X						23
P					X	X	X	X	X				X	X	X	X	X					22
K					X	X	X	X	X	X		X	X	X	X	X	X					21
P					X	X	X	X	X	X		X	X	X	X	X	X					20
K					X	X	X	X	X	X	X	X	X	X	X	X	X					19
P					X	X	X	X	X	X	X	X	X	X	X	X	X					18
K						X	X	X	X	X	X	X	X	X	X	X						17
P						X	X	X	X	X	X	X	X	X	X	X						16
K						X	X	X	X	X	X	X	X	X	X	X						15
P							X	X	X	X	X	X	X	X	X							14
K							X	X	X	X	X	X	X	X	X							13
P								X	X	X	X	X	X	X								12
K								X	X	X	X	X	X	X								11
P										X	X	X										10
K										X	X	X										9
P											X											8
K											X											7
P																						6
K																						5
P																						4
K																						3
P	→																					2
K	←																					1
	1	2	3	4	5	6	7	8	9	10	11	12	13	14	15	16	17	18	19	20	21	

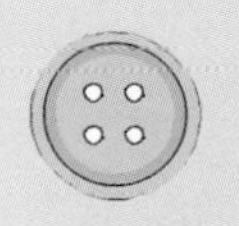

When I'm designing a chart, I like to start the contrasting colour pattern on a knit row. It makes it easier to add the new colour.

Three things to remember when reading a chart:
1. Start reading the chart from the bottom.
2. Knit (RS) rows are read from right to left.
3. Purl (WS) rows are read from left to right.

Note to Knitters

Your knitting pattern will give a key to the squares and symbols on the chart. This key will vary from chart to chart.

Blank knitters' graph paper

Use this to design your own motifs.
Simply photocopy it and start designing!

K																						29
P																						28
K																						27
P																						26
K																						25
P																						24
K																						23
P																						22
K																						21
P																						20
K																						19
P																						18
K																						17
P																						16
K																						15
P																						14
K																						13
P																						12
K																						11
P																						10
K																						9
P																						8
K																						7
P																						6
K																						5
P																						4
K																						3
P	→																					2
K	←																					1
	1	2	3	4	5	6	7	8	9	10	11	12	13	14	15	16	17	18	19	20	21	

Knit and purl motifs

You all know how to knit and purl. These are very basic techniques that you learnt many patterns ago. Now I want to show you how simple combinations of knit and purl can produce far from simple effects. You can use them to create complicated patterns and images, and can even be used to put messages in your knitting. You can use charts to create motifs, and here you can really use your imagination to personalise your knitting.

Rule number one of knitting (see p.38) will be, as always, invaluable with knit and purl patterns. Remember to count your stitches at the end of every row!

Knit and purl motifs

Using the heart chart on p.160 you can work in knit and purl combinations to create any image you like. This is a more subtle way of adding an image into your knitting than colourwork. I've made my image in stocking stitch on a garter stitch background. This makes the pattern stand out nicely, and the knitting will not curl up (so it would be perfect for a scarf, or alternatively a baby's blanket).

This chart is the same as would be used for Swiss darning or intarsia. Follow the key carefully to knit the stocking stitch heart on a garter stitch background.

Use the heart chart but follow this key to knit your heart motif.

☐ = Knit on RS and knit on WS

X = Knit on RS and purl on WS

You can work knit and purl patterns into garments, or make charming little coasters or greetings cards with small squares of knitting.

Handy HINT

The main thing you have to remember is:

When you knit, the yarn is at the back.

When you purl, the yarn is at the front.

Handy HINT

Here is a tip from my test knitters: to keep an eye on the rows, you can use a stitch counter – or do as I do and remember to tick off the rows as you work them. Accuracy is important when following a chart.

Moss zig stitch

This stitch started off as the moss zigzag that I give my advanced beginners to knit to practise their stitch skills. One of these knitters took it a step further and decided that she wanted diagonal stripes rather than a zigzag ... and that's a great example of how you can design your own stitches using only knit and purl. It doesn't take years of knitting to start designing – all you need is an idea and a willingness to experiment!

MOSS ZIG STITCH

Cast on a multiple of 9 stitches (18sts is a good number to practise with).

Row 1 (RS): K4, P1, K1, P1, K1, P1, repeat from beginning to the end of the row.

Row 2 (WS): P1, K1, P1, K1, P1, K1, P3, repeat to end.

Row 3: K2, P1, K1, P1, K1, P1, K2, repeat to end.

Row 4: P3, K1, P1, K1, P1, K1, P1, repeat to end.

Row 5: P1, K1, P1, K1, P1, K4, repeat to end.

Row 6. K1, P4, K1, P1, K1, P1, repeat to end.

Row 7: P1, K1, P1, K4, P1, K1, repeat to end.

Row 8: K1, P1, K1, P4, K1, P1, repeat to end.

Row 9: P1, K4, P1, K1, P1, K1, repeat to end.

Row 10: K1, P1, K1, P1, K1, P4, repeat to end.

Row 11: K3, P1, K1, P1, K1, P1, K1, repeat to end.

Row 12: P2, K1, P1, K1, P1, K1, P2, repeat to end.

Row 13: K1, P1, K1, P1, K1, P1, K3, repeat to end.

Row 14: P4, K1, P1, K1, P1, K1, repeat to end.

Row 15: K1, P1, K1, P1, K4, P1, repeat to end.

Row 16: P1, K1, P4, K1, P1, K1, repeat to end.

Row 17: K1, P1, K4, P1, K1, P1, repeat to end.

Row 18: P1, K1, P1, K1, P4, K1, repeat to end.

Repeat the last 18 rows until the piece is as long as you want it to be, ending on any RS row.

Cast off in pattern on the WS of your work.

For instructions on how to make and finish a knitted cushion cover, see the free PDFs at www.knittingsos.co.uk.

The front of the cushion is moss zig, and the back with the buttons is in moss stitch (K1, P1 on an odd number of stitches).

Fair Isle and intarsia knitting

In Fair Isle and intarsia knitting you use more than one colour in each row to create a design or motif in a piece of stocking stitch knitting.

In Fair Isle, the design is small or intricate and the yarns of various colours are carried behind the work until they are needed.

In intarsia, the motif is worked in bigger blocks of colour to create bolder images, and as it would be impractical to carry the yarn over large areas at the back of the knitting, the yarn is wound on to bobbins for each separate part of the pattern.

You can slip a bit of Fair Isle or intarsia into any piece of stocking stitch knitting. Perhaps you could use it on the border of a cardigan, or turn the Men's bulky jumper (p.60) into a jolly winter pressie, or how about using it to add a bit of zing to a simple hat pattern? You can really unleash your creativity here.

You can use these techniques on any stocking stitch piece of knitting. Here you can see how effective the techniques are on cushion covers. Go to www.knittingsos.co.uk for free instructions on how to finish a knitted cushion cover.

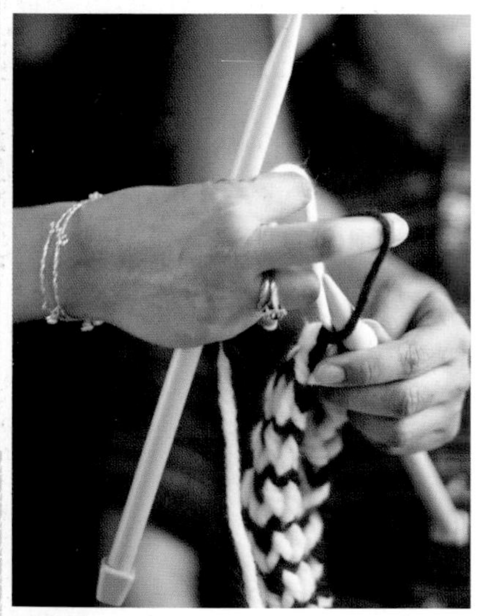

Really practise using two fingers to hold the strands of yarn when knitting Fair Isle – it will be tricky at first, but you'll get the hang of it.

Fair Isle

Try this simple Fair Isle pattern, which uses two colours to create a decorative design. Fair Isle is often worked in the round, but it can be knitted on straight needles too. The yarn is carried over small areas at the back of the work.

KEY

□ = Knit on RS and purl on WS

X = Knit and purl using the contrasting colour

K																					23
P																					22
K																					21
P																					20
K																					19
P																					18
K		X		X		X		X		X		X		X		X		X		X	17
P	X		X		X		X		X		X		X		X		X		X		16
K		X		X		X		X		X		X		X		X		X		X	15
P																					14
K																					13
P																					12
K																					11
P																					10
K	X		X		X		X		X		X		X		X		X		X		9
P		X		X		X		X		X		X		X		X		X		X	8
K	X		X		X		X		X		X		X		X		X		X		7
P																					6
K																					5
P																					4
K																					3
P																					2
K																					1

Work in stocking stitch for 6 rows (starting with a knit row and ending with a purl row) until the start of the Fair Isle section.

For a refresher on how to read a chart, see p.160.

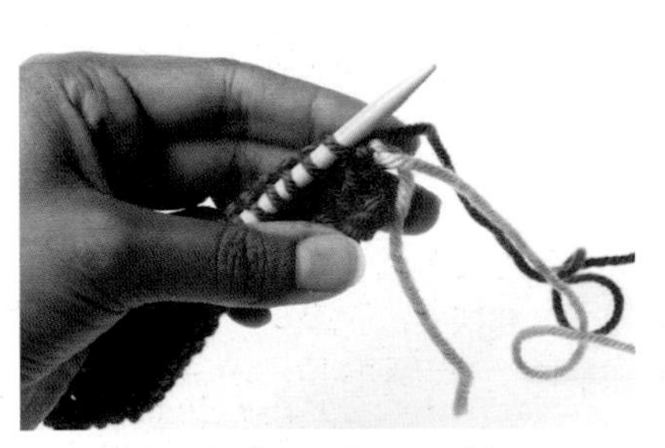

Join the new colour of yarn without cutting the original yarn.

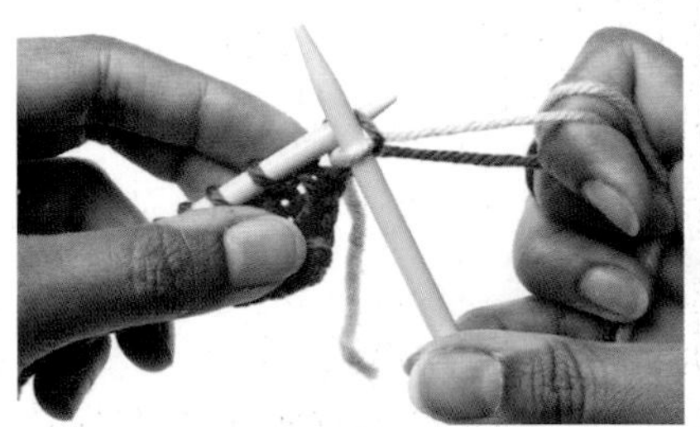

Knit the first stitch in the new colour (following the chart).

Knit the second stitch in the original colour.

Handy HINT

You can wrap each of the two colours of yarn around your right index and middle finger and use each finger to knit in turn. If you find that this is too tricky, simply pick up each colour as you need it. As there is only a small distance between each colour change in Fair Isle, you don't need to worry about twisting the yarns at the back of the work as you work along the row, as you would with intarsia.

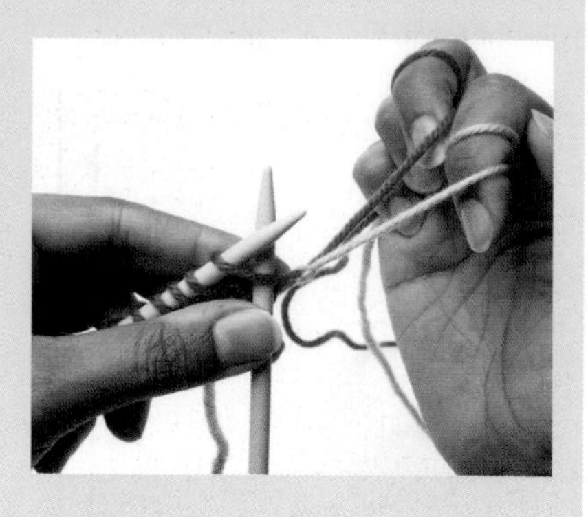

Continue the row, knitting each stitch in a different colour according to the chart.

Here's what your work will look like after the first row of the Fair Isle chart.

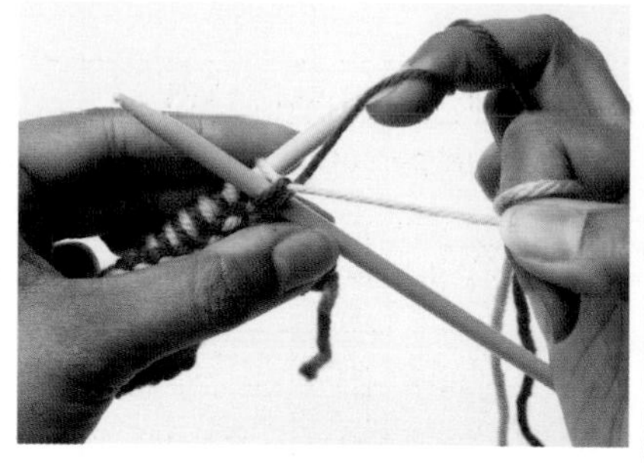

At the start of the next row – the purl row – twist the two strands of yarn at the beginning of the row, at the back of the work.

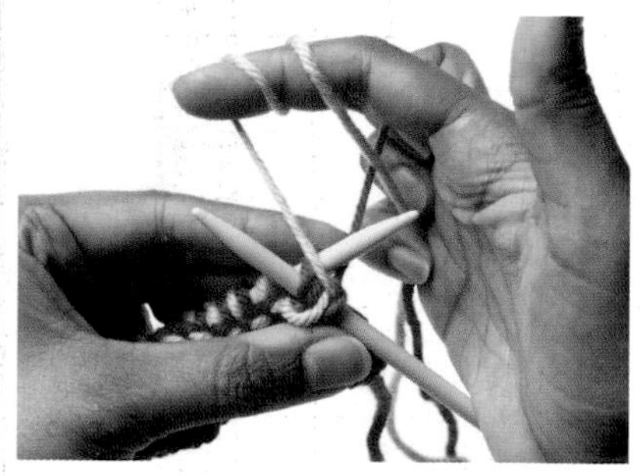

Purl across the row using the opposite colour for each stitch. For example, here I use the blue to purl a pink stitch and vice versa.

Here's how your knitting will look after you've worked a knit row and a purl row of the Fair Isle chart.

There will be a few loose ends at the back of the work where you've joined the new colour. Ensure that you weave these into the back of the work neatly and securely.

Intarsia

For this practice pattern, I drew out a bold shape on knitter's graph paper.

Handy HINT

You have the option of winding small amounts of yarn on to bobbins, but I sometimes find these to be a bit unwieldy and prefer to have long strands of yarn hanging from the back of my knitting. I add more long strands as I need them. I find that this makes for fewer tangles at the back of the work. Have a go with bobbins or long strands and see which you prefer.

Start by winding some of the yarn into separate balls, or on to a bobbin if you wish. This is so you can work each side of the pink background from two different balls of yarn, rather than carrying the yarn across the back of the blue shape, which would be untidy.

KEY

☐ = Knit on RS and purl on WS

X = Knit and purl using the contrasting colour

K																					27
P																					26
K																					25
P																					24
K																					23
P										X	X										22
K									X	X	X	X									21
P								X	X	X	X	X	X								20
K						X	X	X	X	X	X	X	X	X	X						19
P						X	X	X	X	X	X	X	X	X	X						18
K						X	X	X	X	X	X	X	X	X	X						17
P					X	X	X	X	X	X	X	X	X	X	X	X					16
K					X	X	X	X	X	X	X	X	X	X	X	X					15
P					X	X	X	X	X	X	X	X	X	X	X	X					14
K					X	X	X	X	X	X	X	X	X	X	X	X					13
P						X	X	X	X	X	X	X	X	X	X						12
K						X	X	X	X	X	X	X	X	X	X						11
P						X	X	X	X	X	X	X	X	X	X						10
K								X	X	X	X	X	X								9
P									X	X	X	X									8
K										X	X										7
P																					6
K																					5
P																					4
K																					3
P																					2
K																					1
	1	2	3	4	5	6	7	8	9	10	11	12	13	14	15	16	17	18	19	20	

Work until you get to the start of the blue shape and join the blue yarn.

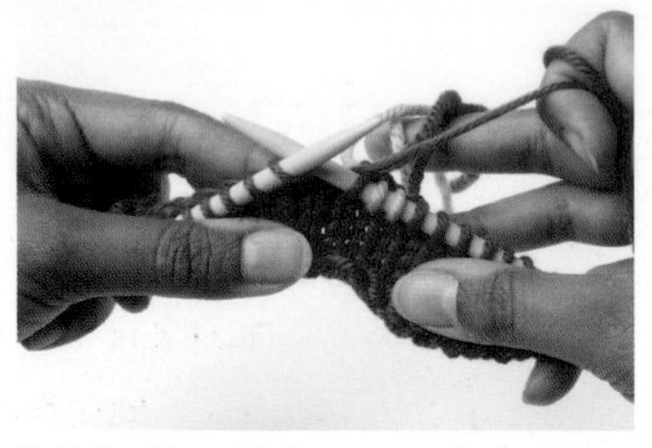

Knit the blue stitches as marked on the chart, then join the pink yarn from the ball that you previously wound into a separate ball.

Complete the row with the pink yarn from the separate ball.

On the next row, purl until you get to the place where the blue starts.

Twist the blue yarn under and then over the pink yarn, and work the next stitches as shown on the chart.

When you get to the next pink section on that row, twist the pink yarn from the other side under and over the blue and work the rest of the row.

Continue working the rows and following the chart, making sure that you twist the yarn every time there is a colour change. You'll soon see the pattern start to emerge.

The back of your work will look quite messy at this stage. Don't worry: we'll sort it out at the end. If, at any stage, the yarn from the separate ball runs out, simply wind off some more yarn and join it in the usual way.

When you get to the end of the blue shape, you can cut one of the pink yarns so that you are now only knitting with one ball of pink again to complete the chart.

When you have finished, you'll see that there are several loose strands of yarn at the back of the work. These loose ends can be neatened by weaving them into the back of the work.

Questions & Answers

Why do I need to twist the yarn at a colour change?

If you don't, there will be a gap in the knitting between the colours. When you knit with a new piece of yarn, you need to make sure you are knitting as if the yarn were joined together for a continuous piece of knitting.

The strands at the back of my work are all tangled!

Don't worry: if you get into too much of a snarl simply cut the yarn, leaving ends long enough to be woven in, and join a new piece of yarn to work with.

Handy HINT

I suggest you leave the loose ends fairly long, so that you can weave them in using a darning needle rather than a crochet hook, as this is a bit easier to do.

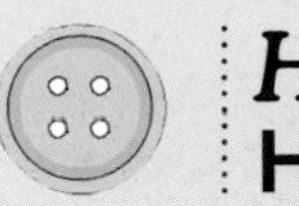

Handy HINT

Take your time over weaving in. My mother always taught me that the inside of your work should be as tidy as the outside – this is good advice for all neat crafters!

Questions & Answers

Help! I forgot to twist the yarn and I have a hole in my knitting.

Don't panic: you can usually correct this by sewing up the hole from the inside. Use loose ends of yarn or matching sewing thread for a subtle repair.

Swiss darning

So this isn't officially knitting, but I couldn't resist including it. Swiss darning isn't seen much these days, but I foresee a comeback for this simple, clever technique for adding colour patterns and motifs into your knitting.

Swiss darning is a way of sewing a colour pattern on to a piece of stocking stitch knitting. It has a similar look to intarsia or Fair Isle, but is infinitely simpler to produce than knitting with all those strands of yarn. Personally, I like the effect of intarsia and Fair Isle, but I really don't enjoy the process and I'm a firm believer that a crafter must enjoy the process as much, if not more, than the final product!

If, like me, you prefer the simple life, try Swiss darning to add colour and pattern to your knitting. You can use it on any stocking stitch knitting. It would work well on a cushion cover, for instance, or on small squares of knitting to turn into greetings cards.

Here I've added a fun bit of Swiss darning to the Gloves on p.90.

You can personalise any stocking stitch knitting, such as the Versatile kiddies' jumper on p.72: add any motif you like!

There are so many possibilities once you master this new technique. Have fun experimenting.

How to do Swiss darning

To start with, you need a plain background of stocking stitch. This practice piece features a heart. Cast on 21sts and work in stocking stitch for 29 rows. End with a RS row and cast off on the WS of the knitting.

Note to Knitters

See p.160 for how to read a chart. The same charts can be used for intarsia, Fair Isle, Swiss darning or Knit and purl motifs.

You are now ready to follow the chart. I suggest that you start from the bottom point of the heart and work your way upwards. If you've ever done counted cross stitch, it's a similar process – each stitch is represented by a square on the chart.

You are going to sew the heart design on top of the stocking stitch background, by following the line of each stitch. The best way to do this is by following the 'V' of the stitch. Each square of the chart is the 'V' of a stitch.

Start by threading the yarn onto a darning needle and pulling it from the back of the work to the front, at the point where you want to start sewing. Leave a long tail at the back and use it for weaving in later.

Pick up the two sides of the 'V' of a stitch just above where you want to start sewing.

Insert the needle back into the point at which you started.

You can see that you've exactly covered the original pink stitch of the background with a blue stitch.

Then work your way up the chart to create the heart motif.

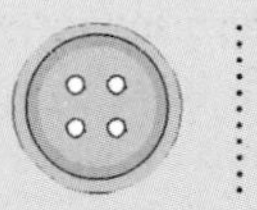

Here's a tip from my testers: you'll find it easier if the background piece of knitting is a light or bright colour. You'll be able to see the structure of the stitches more easily than when working on a very dark background – especially the first time you try this technique.

Sometimes it will be easier to sew if you turn your work to hold it an angle. Don't be afraid to turn your work in all directions to make it easier to sew! Work across each row, making sure you cover the 'V' of each stitch for each square on the chart.

***Handy* HINT**

When you've finished sewing, take care to weave the ends into the back of your work. Try and weave each colour into itself rather than weaving the blue yarn into the pink knitting, for example.

When you've finished your Swiss darning, make sure you take time to weave in all the ends neatly.

Note to Knitters

Be sure to use the same make and model of yarn for the darning as you did for the base square, so it is the same thickness. This will ensure that the darning yarn will cover each stitch neatly.

The stitch-library scarf afghan

Sounds like the title of a novel, eh? But no – it's my way of knitting a blanket or afghan.

New knitters often tell me that they want to knit a blanket out of squares as they think it will be easy. I almost always discourage this! My reasoning is: squares can be dull and samey to knit, and you'll need an awful lot of them; plus the sewing-up process will take forever and never look as tidy as you want. Both of these reasons can be disheartening, and I don't want anyone to be put off knitting due to one badly thought-out project.

So … you still want to knit a blanket? Try what I call my 'scarf-blanket' technique. It has plenty of scope for creativity and personalisation, and it will be much more satisfying to knit and sew up than squares. Another benefit of this technique is that you won't end up lugging around a huge and heavy knitting project, as each scarf is of course very portable.

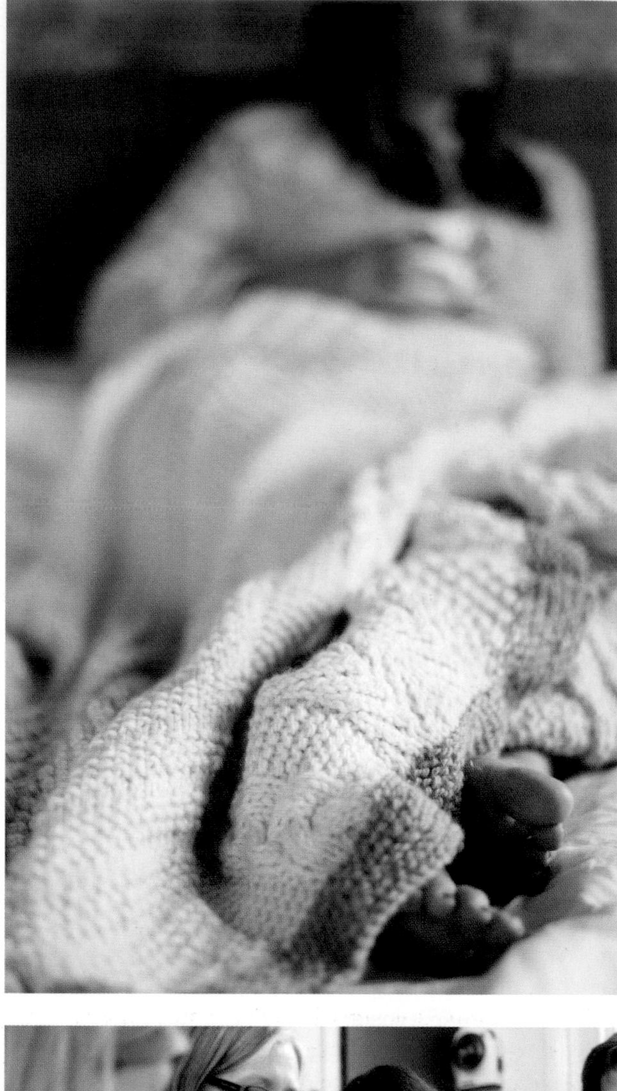

YOU WILL NEED

I suggest a chunky-weight yarn on 7 or 8mm needles, as this will be quicker to knit and warm to snuggle under. I've used Rowan British Sheep Breeds Chunky Undyed, as it comes in lovely natural, neutral shades. I used around 18 balls for this afghan and knitted each scarf to be 150cm long, but of course your blanket can be as big or small as you choose. (You can use the same principles for knitting an afghan on finer yarn and needles to knit a baby blanket.)

Look at the stitch pattern library (or any stitches you fancy) and choose the ones you want in your afghan, then knit some practice squares.

Once you've chosen your stitch patterns, knit several scarves, using one stitch pattern per scarf. Alternatively, mix and match as many or as few stitch patterns in a scarf as you wish, to create the texture of your choice.

I chose to start and finish each side of my scarves with a few rows of contrasting coloured garter stitch, as I wanted the edges to be neat. You could choose to knit a few rows in a stitch or colour of your choice, to work as a border.

This project is ideal for group knitting. If you're knitting this as a gift, you and your friends could knit a scarf each and sew them up into a single blanket. This would make a great gift for a baby shower, a housewarming or to donate to charity.

Making up

Lay out your scarves in the order you like best (I'm not giving you very detailed instructions here as I want this to be designed to your own taste rather than a prescribed pattern), and sew them up along the long edges.

You can use mattress stitch; if you get confused when sewing up all the different stitches, just remember that the general rule of thumb when sewing up with mattress stitch is to look for a horizontal bar on both sides of the knitted fabric.

One of the great things about this pattern is that you can keep adding to your afghan until it's as big as you want!

Farewell and good luck!

Woo hoo! Congratulations. If you've made it this far then you are well on the road to becoming an accomplished knitter, with not just the technical skills to add finesse to your knitting, but the experience and understanding to add flair and creativity to any knitting pattern you choose. I hope you've enjoyed the ride and will use this book as your stepping stone as you travel deeper into the Wonderful World of Knitting.

Appendix

Conversion charts

KNITTING NEEDLE SIZES	
2mm	(UK14/US0)
2.25mm	(UK13/US1)
2.75mm	(UK12/US2)
3mm	(UK11/US n/a)
3.25mm	(UK10/US3)
3.5mm	(UK n/a/US4)
3.75mm	(UK9/US5)
4mm	(UK8/US6)
4.5mm	(UK7/US7)
5mm	(UK6/US8)
5.5mm	(UK5/US9)
6mm	(UK4/US10)
6.5mm	(UK3/US10½)
7mm	(UK2/US n/a)
10mm	(UK000/US15)
12mm	(UK n/a/US17)
15mm	(UK n/a/US n/a)

YARN WEIGHT	
Grams	Ounces
25	0.88
50	1.76
75	2.65
100	3.5
150	5.29
200	7.05
250	8.81

CENTIMETRES TO INCHES	
Centimetres	Inches
1	0.39
5	1.97
10	3.94
15	5.9
20	7.87
25	9.84
30	11.8

METRES TO YARDS	
Metres	Yards
1	1.0936
2	2.1872
5	5.468
10	10.936
25	27.34
50	54.68
75	82.02
100	109.36
500	546.8
1000	1093.6

YARN	
UK	USA
2 Ply	Lace weight
4 Ply	Fingering
Double knit	Sport/Double knit
Aran	Worsted
Chunky	Bulky

Abbreviations

[ ]	Sequence of instructions in square brackets is to be repeated as stated
Approx.	Approximately
Circ	Circular needle
Cont	Continue
Dpn(s)	Double-pointed needle(s)
K	Knit
K2tog	Knit two stitches together
K2tog tbl	Knit two stitches together through the back of the loops
KFB	Knit into the front and back of a stitch
Knitwise	Treat stitches as if you were about to knit them
M1	Make one stitch
P	Purl
P2SSO	Pass two slipped stitches over
P2tog	Purl two stitches together
P2tog tbl	Purl two stitches together through the back of the loops
PB	Place bead
PM	Place/pass marker
Purlwise	Treat stitches as if you were about to purl them
Rem	Remaining
Rib	Work in rib stitch as specified
RS	Right side
SKP	Slip, knit, pass
SKPO	Slip, knit, pass over
Sl	Slip
Sl1P	Slip one stitch purlwise
SM	Slip marker
SSK	Slip, slip, knit
St(s)	Stitch(es)
W&T	Wrap and turn (short row shaping)
WS	Wrong side
YF; YF2; YF3; YF4	Yarn forward: bring the yarn to the front of the work as if you were about to purl it (although next stitch will not necessarily be a purl stitch); yarn forward twice; yarn forward three times; yarn forward four times
YO	Yarn over

Stockists

Artesano www.artesanoyarns.co.uk
Quality yarns from ethical producers.

Colinette www.colinette.com
Beautiful hand-painted luxury yarns.

Debbie Bliss www.debbieblissonline.co.uk
Gorgeous yarns, stylish patterns and more!

Get Knitted www.getknitted.com
Terrific shop and online store with some hard-to-find yarns as well as all the favourites, and knitting accessories.

HCS Crafts www.hcscrafts.co.uk
Family-run craft store. Great for bulk buys for craft groups.

Hip Knits www.hipknits.co.uk
Luxurious hand-painted yarns and fibres.

I Knit London www.iknit.org.uk
Shop and sanctuary for knitters.

John Lewis www.johnlewis.com
Good selection of favourite yarns and accessories.

Loop www.loopknittingcom
London yarn boutique with knitting supplies sourced from all over the world.

Prick Your Finger www.prickyourfinger.com
Yarn shop and gallery in East London specialising in natural and hand-spun fibres.

Rowan www.knitrowan.com
Yarns, patterns, knitting books, workshops and much more.

Sirdar www.sirdar.co.uk
A terrific source for yarn and accessories – look out for their amazing novelty yarn selection.

Stylecraft www.stylecraft-yarns.co.uk
Yarns and patterns to suit all tastes.

Yarnbox www.yarnbox.co.uk
Online shop for beautiful yarns and accessories.

Yarnscape www.yarnscape.co.uk
Luxurious hand-spun and hand-dyed yarns.

Index